CW01021921

PRAISE FOR
THE BARTENDER'S ULTIMATE GUIDE TO COCKTAILS

"This book is a toboggan ride through the history of the cocktail. Packed with wonderful facts and nuggets at every turn. Cheryl has mined some of the leading experts to come up with a compelling story."

—Dale "King Cocktail" DeGroff, *The Craft of the Cocktail* and *The Essential Cocktail*

"Cheryl has demystified the cocktail, and made it what it should always be: fun and approachable! She takes us on an entertaining journey into the world of libations and those who serve them; their histories, stories, and antidotes. In the end, we better understand how we have arrived where we are and leave a more educated and appreciative imbiber!"

—Tony Abou-Ganim, *The Modern Mixologist*

"Eureka! Cheryl Charming just made the internet obsolete. The bartending maven once again has done all the digging and delivered the gold on the history of everything bartending, cocktails, and cocktail bars."

—Tobin Ellis, BarMagic of Las Vegas

"Cheryl Charming makes facts fun again! In addition to page-turning chapters on drink evolution through the millennia and the backstory of just about every famous cocktail. This book offers thoroughly entertaining sections on cocktails in film, literature, and television."

—Jeff "Beachbum" Berry, *Sippin' Safari*; *Beachbum Berry's Intoxica!*; *Beach Bum Berry's Remixed*; *Beach Bum Berry's Grog Log*; and *Beach Bum Berry's Taboo Table*

THE BARTENDER'S
ULTIMATE GUIDE
TO COCKTAILS

THE BARTENDER'S
ULTIMATE GUIDE
TO COCKTAILS

Alcohol Lore, Cocktail Culture,
Drink Recipes and More

CHERYL CHARMING

CORAL GABLES

You know how it is. You pick up a book, flip to the dedication, and find that, once again, the author has dedicated a book to someone else and not to you. Not this time. This one's for you. With you know what, and you probably know why, and with a cocktail in hand.

www.misscharming.com

CONTENTS

FOREWORD

In her inimitable fashion, Miss Charming, the bartender who is considered by many, myself included, to be the ultimate Queen of the New Orleans Cocktail Scene, has delivered yet another fabulous book, chock-full of all manner of cocktailian splendor. And this one's a doozy!

The world of cocktails flows with fascinating trivia, incredible folklore, accurate historical stories, some tall tales, and lots of straight, hard facts. I believe that Cheryl Charming has detailed near-as-darn-it every single one of these pearls of liquid wisdom in this tome. Skim through it for a few minutes and see how much time passes before you can even dream of putting it down.

Who else would describe garnishes as jewelry for cocktails? Nobody. That's who. It's part of Cheryl's unique style, and it's part of what makes her stand out in any crowd of cocktail aficionados. This book will walk you through drinking scenes from movies, books, and television.

You'll find, too, that Cheryl goes the whole nine yards when it comes to research. Fancy a Ramos Gin Fizz, for instance? You'll find that a certain Henry Charles "Carl" Ramos invented the drink in 1888 and his bar went through an incredible 5,000 eggs every week to keep up with demand for the drink.

But Cheryl doesn't stop there. Read on and she'll tell you where to get the best Ramos Gin Fizzes in New Orleans today, and I wasn't surprised to see that Bourbon O Bar, where Miss Charming struts her stuff, is one of them. I've had a Ramos Gin Fizz at the Bourbon "O" Bar. It was sublime.

When was the first golden age of the cocktail? Which family has been producing fine apple brandy in New Jersey since the late 1600s? When were cocktails first served on an aircraft? (Far earlier than you're thinking.) Where can you find a cocktail that incorporates crushed Mexican black ants? Which cocktail should be shaken to the rhythm of the Foxtrot?

All this and more will be revealed to you in this great book.

And buyer beware: if you loan this book to a friend, you might never see it again.

—gaz regan

STEP UP TO THE BAR:
AN ALCOHOL TIMELINE

No one knows the exact date when cocktails started, but through archeological findings, it is assumed that humans have been mixing ingredients together to create tasty beverages for themselves for 10,000 years because that is when domestic agriculture began—and if you believe in the Lost Continent then it goes back even further. Mead (made from honey), ale (beer), and wine (made from fruit) are the most common alcoholic drinks found in ancient civilizations, so it is also assumed that these ingredients were mixed together to create honey-flavored beverages. In addition, it is imagined that herbs and spices were thrown in to infuse more flavor, and possibly steeped medicinal herbs were used on occasion. Social drinking has been part of every culture in some form and with time, people began to travel (for various reasons) and needed shelter, so humble inns along their path provided temporary housing, food, and drink—the same basic amenities modern hotels provide today. Public houses (pubs) were built in towns and served as "information hubs" where you learned of current events, gossiped, complained about the weather, flirted, told stories, and, of course, drank. Things pretty much remained the same for hundreds of years.

There have been many theories of where the word "cocktail" came from. Some include an Aztec princess, an Ancient Roman doctor who called a favorite drink cockwine, a New Orleans French egg cup, Cock Ale Punch that was actually made with a whole rooster and ale (ick!), a gingerroot suppository for a non-spirited horse, and a tavern keeper who put rooster tail feathers in soldiers' drinks (cock-tail).

The first known reference to the Asian spirit "arrack" was by traveling merchants in the 1200s. In the 1300s the word "aqua vitae" ("water of life") was coined and Armagnac and Scotch whisky were being produced in the 1400s. But the first record of a spirit (an early rum) being mixed with three other ingredients in bulk was for ill sailors in the 1500s. Between the 1600s and 1800s, communal drinks were served in big bowls—with cups for all. These cups and bowls gave birth to the individual-sized cocktail we know today.

The Top Ten Things to Know about Cocktails

1. No one knows who invented the cocktail, but it is agreed that communal batches served in punch bowls then drank from cups in the 1600s gave birth to the individual cocktail we know today.

2. There have been many theories about the origin of the word "cocktail." As of today, it has been narrowed down to two. One comes from a 1700s word in the horse trade profession, and the other from a fictional character based on a real person, but neither has been confirmed.

3. To date, the first printed form of the word "cocktail" appeared in 1798. The word pertaining to the drink was first printed in 1803 and the first printed definition was in 1806.

4. The first known British drink receipt (recipe) book was published in 1827. The first known American cocktail recipe book was published in 1862.

5. As far as we know, the Mint Julep is America's first cocktail.

6. Before the 1920s, in America, fancy cocktails were drunk by prominent white males in fancy saloons and bars. The average joe drank beer, wine, whiskey, and cider at pubs, while a fancy bar might have a side room for fancy women called the "Ladies' Bar." The only women allowed in the main bar were madams and prostitutes.

7. The first golden age of the cocktail was between 1860 and 1919, and the seed for the second golden age of the cocktail was planted around the millennium.

8. The Martini is the most iconic cocktail and symbol of the cocktail culture.

9. The repeal of the American Prohibition, women's freedom to socialize in most bars, and Hollywood technology (talkies) glamorized cocktails between the 1930s and 1960s.

10. The world's largest cocktail festival, Tales of the Cocktail, has been held in New Orleans each July since 2002.

A COCKTAIL TIMELINE

1500S

If you owned a pub, alehouse, tavern, or inn, you were probably growing your own food for meals and drink to serve guests. In addition to having land for a garden, you needed to tend to animals, provide stables for travelers (we call them parking lots today), have an area to produce alcoholic drink, and be literate enough to keep books, pay bills, manage help, and collect payments. Tavern floors were often made of sand, and it was common to have a portcullis (metal vertical closing gate) around the bar area. To multitask dinner, a kitchen dog was often placed in a turnspit wheel—the dog would walk inside the wheel, which slowly turned meat roasting over a fire.

Names of alehouses, pubs, taverns, and inns included Beverley Arms, Black Lion, Boar's Head, Bull Long Medford, Crown Sarre, King's Head, the Crane Inn, the Devil's Tavern, the George, the Lion, the Prospect of Whitby, the White Horse, and Ye Olde Mitre.

Drinking words heard were "aled up," "befuddled," "bizzled," "drinking deep," "has on a barley cap," "has more than one can hold," "lion drunk," "malt above the meal," "rowdy," "swallowed a tavern token," "shattered," "shaved," "swilled up," "wassailed," and "whittled."

New brands and spirits created in the 1500s included aguardiente de caña (rum), brandy, cachaça, Disarrono, jenever, kummel, mezcal, pisco, and Scotch whiskey.

1500 – Sugarcane is harvested in Hispaniola to be used to make rum.

– Scotland's King James IV grants the production of aqua vitae.

1514 – King Louis XII of France licenses vinegar producers to distill eau-de-vie.

1518 – Spanish ruler Charles V imports 2,000 slaves to Hispaniola to work the sugarcane fields.

1525 – Amaretto Disaronno is produced in Italy.

– A groundbreaking distilling book is published and inspires Holland to produce brandewijn (burnt wine).

1531 – Spanish settlers distill the local fermented drink in Mexico to make mexcalli (mezcal).

1533 – Sugarcane eau-de-vie is created (later known as cachaça).

– Monks in the Italian mountains make liqueurs.

1534 – A book with over seventy vodka-based medicines is published. It is the first time the word "vodka" is documented.

1537 – King Francis I of France grants the production of eau-de-vie.

1538 – Peruvian farmers make what we know today as pisco.

1552 – In the book *Constelijck Distilleer Boek*, Philippus Hermanni refers to a juniper-infused eau-de-vie in his 1568.

1575 – Lucas Bols sets up a distillery in Amsterdam and begins making jenever.

1586 – Aguardiente de caña (basically, rum), *hierba buena* (Cuban herbal plant that belongs to the mint family), limes, and sugar were batched for a ship of sick sailors and its British sea captain, Sir Francis Drake (nicknamed El Draque—Spanish for "the dragon"). All that was needed was an addition of fizzy water and they'd have had themselves a barrel of Mojitos.

1600S

We have a good idea of what taverns and pubs looked like because Dutch painter Jan Steen painted detailed daily life paintings. His paintings related to drinking include *Prince's Day in a Tavern* (1660; he painted himself in the painting), *Tavern Garden* (1660), *In the Tavern* (1660), *The Drinker* (1660), *A Merry Party* (1660), *Peasants Before an Inn* (1653), *Leaving the Tavern* (unknown date), *Merry Company on a Terrace* (1670), and *Tavern Scene* (1670). Things seen in Steen's paintings are jugs, bottles, vessels (some made of glass), sheet music, musical instruments, flirting, fire, food, laughter, games, gambling, animals, children, toys, messes, men grabbing women, smoking, skulls, barrels, and birds in cages. Minus the children and animals, this is pretty much what is seen in modern bars. My personal favorite painting is titled *As the Old Sing, so Pipe the Young* (1668).

In the early 1600s, punch (paunch, a Hindu word that means "five") became popular among English sailors and spice merchants who would travel to India and back. While sailing homeward, they would make big bowls of punch with five ingredients, including spirit, lemon, sugar, water, and spice. Punch spread to Britain's upper class, and it was soon taken to the New World (America). The upper class owned bowls, cups, and ladles made of silver, and records in London's Central Criminal Court documented many incidents of these items being stolen—most times with the punch still in the bowl!

As for Pilgrims who sought a new life in the New World, life was hard carving out an uncharted land while depending on English ships for supplies. For the most part, settlers were in survival mode, but somehow they found the time and resources to open not one but two rum distilleries. Rum is what funded early America.

Some names of alehouses, pubs, taverns, and inns included Bear at Bridge-foot, Bull and Bush, Bull and Gate, Grapes, Green Dragon Tavern, Hatchet Inn, the Anchor, the Plough, the Red Lion, the Seven Stars, Three Nuns, and Trafalgar Tavern.

Drinking words heard in the 1600s included "admiral of the narrow seas," "beastly drunk," "boozed," "bubbled cap-sick," "caught a fox," "D and D" (drunk and disorderly), "dull in the eye," "elevated," "giggled up," "got bread and cheese in one's head," "muddled up," "on a continual drinking merry-go-round," "on the rampage," and "seeing double."

New brands and spirits in the 1600s include Bushmills Irish whiskey, Chartreuse, and Haig Scotch.

Prince's Day in a Tavern, by Jan Steen, 1660, Dutch painting, oil on panel. Prince's Day was a birthday celebration in honor of Prince William III of Orange-Nassau (November 14, 1660). © *Everett Art / Shutterstock*

1608 – Old Bushmills Distillery is established in Ireland. Today it holds the title of the first licensed whiskey distillery in the world.

1620 – The Pilgrims bring brandy and gin with them on the *Mayflower* to the New World on November 9. The 101 brave colonists live aboard the ship in the winter and supplies run low quickly.

1623 – Jenever is mentioned in the English play *The Duke of Milan*.

1625 – Haig becomes the first recognized Scotch whisky.

1635 – Portuguese government prohibits the sale of cachaça. The ban is lifted in 1695.

1637 – Distillery equipment is brought to the island of Barbados.

1644 – Distillery equipment is brought to the island of Martinique.

1657 – A rum distillery is built in Boston.

1664 – A rum distillery is built in New York City.

1650 – To save room, Admiral Robert Blake switches beer rations with brandy.

1655 – Vice Admiral William Penn orders rum be included in daily rations.

1660 – Popular and cocky punch maker Billy "Bully" Dawson says, "The man who sees, does, or thinks of anything else while he is making punch may as well look for the Northwest Passage on Mutton Hill. A man can never make good punch unless he is satisfied, nay positive, that no man breathing can make better."

1668 – In London's Criminal Court, Thomas Carey is found guilty of stealing punch and its bowl.

1674 – Harvard University builds its own brewhouse.

1676 – When visiting India, physician John Fryer mentions punch that the English make with liquor.

1688 – William of Orange imports jenever from Holland and starts producing British gin.

1691 – Nolet begins to distill in Holland. (They later produce Ketel One Vodka.)

1694 – On Christmas Day, English Navy commander Admiral Edward Russell fills a blue-and-white-tiled fountain with punch and throws a party for 6,000 people in the Spanish port of Cadiz. He hires 800 staff and 1 male child in a boat afloat the punch, serving guests.

1695 – DeKuyker opens a distillery in Holland.

1697 – A fancy British punch bowl is created. They call it Monteith.

1698 – In New Jersey, William Laird begins production of Laird's applejack for personal use.

1699 – Kenelm Digby published *The Closet of Sir Kenelm Digby Knight Opened*, which gives many wine and ale recipes. One recipe in particular is called Cock Ale. Digby says, "These are tame days when we have forgotten how to make Cock Ale." This ale takes a month to make and boiling a rooster is involved. This is the first known reference to Cock Ale. It is seen later in a couple of 1700s cooking books.

1700S

Colonial America was settling into its new home. By 1700, the population reached 275,000 (with Boston and New York City having the highest populations). In 1700, there also were over 140 rum distilleries in the colonies. By the end of the century, the population reached 5.3 million, of which 1 million was of African descent.

In this century, the colonists struggled to break free of Britain. Examples of the old country not wanting to let loose include the Molasses Act (taxing the rum), the Wool Act, the Iron Act, the Currency Act, the Sugar Act (taxing the rum), the Stamp Act, the Boston Massacre, and the Boston Tea Party. This all led to the American Revolution (1775–1783). After breaking off from England, a drink called Sling became popular. It was simply made with a spirit of your choice, sugar, and water. Later, a dash or two of bitters was added making it a Bittered Sling, which was considered a good drink for the morning. These are the exact ingredients for an Old-Fashioned.

The signing of the United States Declaration of Independence in 1776 was toasted with Madeira. Benjamin Franklin wrote a drinking dictionary, invented bifocals, and discovered electricity. James Hargreaves invented the spinning wheel. American whiskey distilleries began to pop up, the sandwich was invented, and for fun, the hot air balloon took its first flight in 1782. On the other side of the pond, the Industrial Revolution was leading the race in textile production, steam power, and iron making, but losing the battle on gin addiction. This was also the century absinthe was discovered.

Often postal service sections were set up in taverns starting in the mid-1700s. Some names of alehouses, pubs, taverns, and inns included Beetle and Wedge, Bell in Hand Tavern, City Tavern, Fraunces Tavern, Jean Lafitte's Blacksmith Shop, Jessop's Tavern, the Stag and Hounds, the Eagle, the Lamb, the Dirty Duck, the Green Man, the Crown, the Old Ship, the Publik House, Prospect of Whitby, Wiggin's Tavern, Blue Bell Inn, and O'Malley's Pub.

Drinking words heard in the 1700s are too many to mention because Benjamin Franklin wrote a 1737 book—by candlelight—titled *The Drinker's Dictionary*, which listed over 200 drinking words. Some of these and others include "addled," "been at Barbados," "cockadoodled," "cherry merry," "cracked," "cranked," "clips the King's English," "dizzy as a coot," "drinking like a fish," "drunk as a wheel barrow," "fears no man," "fuddled up," "full as a goat," "got a snootful," "groggy," "happy juiced," "head full of bees," "in the altitudes," "jacked up," "jolly," "juiced to the gills," "lapping it up," "lost his rudder," "rotten drunk," "screwed and tattooed," "tipsy," and "stewed."

New brands and spirits in the world include absinthe, Admiral Nelson rum, Appleton rum, Cruzan rum, Drambuie, Evan William's whiskey, Gordon's gin, Harvey's Bristol Cream Sherry, Jose Cuervo, Laird's applejack, and Madeira.

1708 – The poem "Old King Cole" describes the king asking for his pipe, bowl (punch bowl), and musicians: "Old King Cole was a merry old soul, and a merry old soul was he; He called for his pipe, and he called for his bowl, and he called for his fiddlers three."

1712 – The first known bitters is created and patented by Richard Staughton.

1717 – The Colt Neck Inn in New Jersey is opened by a William Laird descendant and sells applejack for the first time.

1718 – The French founded New Orleans. Within one hundred years, French-influenced cocktails would be created.

1721 – A quarter of the city of London is used to produce gin.

1726 – London has over 6,000 places to purchase gin.

1727 – Eliza Smith publishes *The Compleat Housewife: Or, Accomplish'd Gentlewoman's Companion* in London. Eighteen editions are produced in fifty years. The book contains hundreds of household receipts (recipes) including many wines, cordials, and a Milk Punch recipe: "To make fine Milk Punch. Take two quarts of water, one quart of milk, half a pint of lemon juice, and one quart of brandy, sugar to your taste; put the milk and water together a little warm, then the sugar, then the lemon juice, stir it well together, then the brandy, stir it again and run it through a flannel bag till 'tis very fine, then bottle it; it will keep a fortnight, or more." Smith also gives a recipe for Cock Ale Punch using an old rooster. The recipe will probably churn even the stomachs of today's flesh-purchasing humans since they are used to the product being wrapped in shiny plastic, so it is not described here, but can be googled if so desired.

1732 – America's first angling club—and the oldest continuous club today—is called "Colony in Schuylkill." (Today it's called Schuylkill Fishing Company of Pennsylvania.) The goal of the club is to socialize, fish, eat, and drink. The famous "Fish House Punch" is created here with a mixture of rum, peach brandy, lemon, sugar, and water. President George Washington is an honoree member.

1734 – On December 4, a mention of arrack punch is mentioned in London's Central Criminal Court: "Mrs. Holcomb came in a Coach to my Door about 2 o'clock in the Morning: I shew'd 'em up two Pair of Stairs, and they had a Bowl—it was but one Bowl—of Arrack Punch, a Bottle of Wine, and three Jellies."

1735 — Arrack punch is mentioned again in London's Central Criminal Court: "He asked me to drink a Glass of Punch, and so I went in, and he and I drank four or five Bowls of Arrack Punch, which came to 20 s. and three Pints of Wine."
Court: What! Did you two drink all that?

— There are too many London's Central Criminal Court documents to mention; almost every available alcohol at the time was mentioned. View them online at oldbaileyonline.org. The most shocking and saddest document shows how addicted England was to gin; on February 27, 1734, a mother kills her two-year-old baby girl so she can sell her clothes to buy gin.

1736 — The Gin Act is passed in England to curb the consumption of gin.

1740 — Is grog the first Daiquiri? On August 21, fifty-five-year-old Vice Admiral Edward Vernon of the Royal Navy issues an order that the daily rum ration should be mixed every day with a quart of water, half pint of rum, lime juice, and sugar mixed in a scuttled butt on the deck in the presence of the Lieutenant of the Watch. (Vernon's nickname was "Old Grog" because of the waterproof cloak he would wear on deck, which was made of grogram cloth. The sailors named the drink "Grog.") Well, grog appears to have the same ingredients of a classic Daiquiri—just without the ice. Before you pull out your cell phone and google "scuttled butt," it was equivalent to the modern-day office water cooler but made out of a wooden cask (barrel) that sailors gathered around. A hole was cut on top to allow the grog to be served to each man.

1742 — Eliza Smith publishes the first known American cookery recipe book. It is the fifth edition of *The Compleat Housewife: Or, Accomplish'd Gentlewoman's Companion*

1743 — The Glenmorangie distillery is established in Scotland.

1744 — A man visiting Philadelphia named William Black records in his diary that he was given:

— "Cider and punch for lunch; rum and brandy before dinner; punch, Madeira, port, and sherry at dinner; punch and liqueurs with the ladies; and wine, spirit, and punch till bedtime; all in punch bowls big enough for a goose to swim in."

1745 – Drambuie is produced in Scotland. The most popular modern cocktail made with Drambuie is the Rusty Nail.

1749 – Appleton rum is produced in Jamaica.
– J&B Scotch is produced.

1751 – England passes another Gin Act.
– The first health warning is printed on a bottle of gin.

1755 – The Marie Brizard Company is founded in Bordeaux, France.

1757 – The first U.S. president, George Washington, writes about his personal beer recipe and titles it "To Make Small Beer."

1758 – Admiral Nelson's Premium Rum is produced.
– George Washington campaigns with a barrel of Barbados rum.
– Don Jose Cuervo receives a land grant to cultivate agave plants in Mexico.

1759 – Arthur Guinness signs a 9,000-year lease on an unused brewery at St. James's Gate in Dublin.

1760 – George Washington is introduced to Laird's applejack.
– Cruzan Rum from the Virgin Islands is produced.

1761 – Bombay Gin from England is produced.

1765 – Richard Hennessy founds Hennessy Cognac.

1769 – Gordon's gin is produced. Gordon's gin will be mentioned in the first James Bond novel, 1953's *Casino Royale*, when Bond orders a Vesper.
– The Henriod sisters advertise their elixir d'absinthe.

1771 – Evan Shelby opens the first rye whiskey distillery in Tennessee.
– Discoveries on how to create carbonated water are documented.

1780 – Jacob Beam builds a whiskey distillery in Kentucky.
– John Jameson opens a whiskey distillery in Dublin, Ireland.
– Johann Tobias Lowitz develops charcoal filtration for vodka.
– Elijah Pepper builds a log cabin distillery in Kentucky.

1783 – Evan Williams Bourbon is produced.

1784 – Philadelphia physician and politician Benjamin Rush publishes a pamphlet titled *An Inquiry into the Effects of Spirituous Liquors on the Human Mind and Body*.

1786 – Antonio Carpano invents vermouth in Italy.

1789 – Reverend Elijah Craig ages corn whiskey in charred oak barrels in Kentucky.
– The first temperance society forms in Litchfield County, Connecticut.

1790	– Jean-Jacob Schweppe makes artificial mineral water.
1791	– George Washington imposes a whiskey tax.
1792	– Pernod absinthe is produced.
1795	– Old Jake Beam Sour Mash whiskey is introduced.
1796	– Harvey's Bristol Cream Sherry is produced.
1791	– George Washington becomes a whiskey distiller.
1798	– Anistatia Miller and Jared Brown are credited with finding the most current recording of the word "cocktail." On Friday, March 16, the *Morning Post and Gazette* in London, England, reported that a pub owner won a lottery and erased all his customers' debts:

> A publican, in Downing-street, who had a share of the 20,000 l. prize, rubbed out all his scores, in a transport of joy: This was a humble imitation of his neighbor, who, when he drew the highest prize in the State Lottery, not only rubbed out, but actually broke scores with his old customers, and entirely forgot them.

– Four days later, on Tuesday, March 20, the customer's debts were published in the same newspapers. The word "cocktail" appears:

"Mr. Pitt, two petit vers of "L'huile de Venus"

Ditto, one of "perfeit amour."

Ditto, "cock-tail." (Vulgarly called ginger.)

– Esteemed spirits and drink historian David Wondrich is of the opinion that the usage of the word "cocktail" (at this time) came from the horse trade. He learned that to make an older horse you were trying to sell look frisky, one would use a chunk of ginger (probably peeled) as a suppository that would cock up the horse's tail.

– The cocktail John Collins is invented in London.

1800S

Cocktails and cocktail making took the stage with a bright white spotlight in the 1800s and American bartenders were the cocktail stars of the whole world. They wore pressed jackets, diamond tiepins, crisp collared shirts; basically, they dressed to the nines. The first recipe books were published, the availability of pond ice (and later, artificial ice) were game changers, and the golden age of the cocktail shone the brightest it has to date. The position of a bartender—even though blue collar—was seen as the aristocracy of the working class. In those days, you had to be a bartender apprentice for several years before you could be a bartender.

One celebrity bartender, Jerry Thomas, traveled the world with a set of solid silver bar tools and he published the first known American cocktail recipe book, *Bar-Tender's Guide, How to Mix Drinks, or the Bon-Vivant's Companion* in 1862.

This century began with an American population of around five million and by 1899 unbelievably increased to a staggering seventy million. Much advancement happened during this time that laid the foundation for the next century. This included gas lighting, sewing machines, the telegraph, Morse code, bicycles, typewriters, mail order catalogs, Coca-Cola, matchbooks, and ice delivery. Moreover, like always, only the wealthy were able to enjoy these modern inventions in the beginning.

These times brought on civilized behavior with new technological advances. A prominent white man at a fancy bar could order a cobbler, crusta, flip, grog, Champagne Cocktail, Manhattan, Earthquake, Martinez, Old-Fashioned, Hailstorm, Rob Roy, Tom & Jerry, Snow-Storm, Roffignac, Eye-Opener, Ramos Gin Fizz, Sazerac, Santa Cruz Punch, smash, Stone-Fence, sour, toddy, or Tom Collins.

Some names of alehouses, taverns, saloons, and bars include Bull and Mouth, Bush Tavern, Chapter House, Crystal Palace Saloon, Golden Cross, Grove House Tavern, Hustler's Tavern, Jack's Elixir Bar, Knickerbocker Saloon, Iron Door Saloon, McSorley's Old Ale House, Old Absinthe House, Pete's Tavern, the Bucket of Blood, the Cock Tavern, the Imperial Cabinet, the Stag Saloon, the Village Tavern, Tujague's, Occidental, and White Horse Tavern.

Drinking words heard in the 1800s include "above par," "a bit on," "a couple of chapters into the novel," "a cup too much," "a date with John Barleycorn," "a drop too much," "a little in the suds," "a public mess," "a spur in the head," "at peace with the floor," "been looking through a glass," "banged up on sauce," "can't see a hole in a ladder," "corked," "dead to the world," "doped up," "drunk as Bacchus," "drunk as forty billy goats," "feeling glorious," "fired up," "fog driver," "full to the brim," "ginned," "lifting the little finger," "lushed," "moonshined," "off the deep end," "moistening the clay," "of flip & c," "phlegm-cutter," "piece of bread and cheese in the attic," "polished," "quenching a spark in the throat," "sloshed," "stinking," "soaked," "swazzled," "tanked," "wetting the whistle," "woozy," and "whacked out of one's skull."

New brands and spirits launched include Averna, Black & White Scotch, Beefeater gin, Boodles gin, Canadian Club whisky, Cherry Heering, Don Q rum, Galliano, George Dickel whiskey, Grand Marnier, Johnnie Walker Scotch, Herradura tequila, Pimm's No. 1, Rose's lime juice, Sauza tequila, Seagram's 7 whisky, vermouth, Seagram's VO whiskey, Tanqueray gin, Fundador Spanish brandy, Lillet, Myers's dark rum, and Lemon Hart rum.

1801   – Chivas Regal Scotch is produced.

1803   – On April 28, the first known American recorded use of the word "cocktail" as a beverage appeared in New Hampshire's newspaper the *Farmer's Cabinet*:

    – "Drank a glass of cocktail—excellent for the head...Call'd at the Doct's. found Burnham—he looked very wise—drank another glass of cocktail."

1806   – The second American recorded use of the word "cocktail" as a beverage appeared in Hudson, New York's the *Balance and Columbian Repository* (No. 18 Vol. V) on May 6:Rum! Rum! Rum!

    It is conjectured, that the price of this precious liquor will soon rife at Claverack since a certain candidate has placed in his account of Loss and Gain, the following items:

    Loss. 720 rum-grogs, 17 brandy do., 32 gin-slings, 411 glasses bitters, 25 do. Cock-tail

    My election.

    Gain. NOTHING.

    – There was an election in Claverack, New York, and it was common (in those days) to try to win votes with free booze. The loser published his Loss and Gains in this local newspaper. Translation for 25 do. = $25 and $25 = $600 in 2017.

    – Seven days later, the newspaper's twenty-eight-year-old editor, Harry Croswell of Columbia County, New York, publishes the "first definition of cocktail" known to be an alcoholic beverage—to date—on May 13. Croswell rarely publishes anything he says but makes an exception this time to answer a question from a subscriber.

    – The subscriber writes:

    To the Editor of the *Balance*:

    Sir,

    I observe in your paper of the 6th instant, in the account of a democratic candidate for a seat in the legislature, marked under the head of Loss, 25 do. cock-tail. Will you be so obliging as to inform me what is meant by this species of refreshment? Though a stranger to you, I believe, from your general character, you will not suppose this request to be impertinent. I have heard of a forum, of phlegm-cutter and fog driver, of wetting the whistle, of moistening the clay, of a fillip, a spur in the head, quenching a spark in the throat, of flip

&c, but never in my life, though have lived a good many years, did I hear of cock-tail before. Is it peculiar to a part of this country? Or is it a late invention? Is the name expressive of the effect which the drink has on a particular part of the body? Or does it signify that the democrats who take the potion are turned topsycurvy, and have their heads where their tails should be? I should think the latter to be the real solution; but am unwilling to determine finally until I receive all the information in my power.

At the beginning of the revolution, a physician publicly recommended the moss which grew on a tree as a substitute for tea. He found on experiment, that it had more of a stimulating quality than he approved; and therefore, he afterward as publicly denounced it. Whatever cock-tail is, it may be properly administered only at certain times and to certain constitutions. A few years ago, when the democrats were bawling for Jefferson and Clinton, one of the polls was held in the city of New York at a place where ice cream was sold. Their temperament then was remarkably adjust and bilious. Something was necessary to cool them. Now when they are sunk into rigidity, it might be equally necessary, by cock-tail to warm and rouse them. I hope you will construe nothing that I have said as disrespectful. I read your paper with great pleasure and wish it the most extensive circulation. Whether you answer my inquiry or not, I shall still remain,

Yours,

A SUBSCRIBER

– Croswell answers the subscriber's question of wanting to know what is the refreshment called cock-tail, while at the same time making fun of politics:

As I make it a point, never to publish anything (under my editorial head) but which I can explain, I shall not hesitate to gratify the curiosity of my inquisitive correspondent: Cock-tail, then in a stimulating liquor, composed of spirits of any kind, sugar, water, and bitters it is vulgarly called a Bittered Sling, and is supposed to be an excellent electioneering potion inasmuch as it renders the heart stout and bold, at the same time that it fuddles the head. It is said also, to be of great use to a democratic candidate: because, a person having swallowed a glass of it, is ready to swallow anything else.

1809 – Washington Irving writes, "This class of beverages originated in Maryland, whose inhabitants were prone to make merry and get fuddled with mint-julep and apple toddy. They were moreover, great horse-racers and cock-fighters; mighty wrestlers and jumpers, and enormous consumers of hoecake and bacon. They lay claim to be the first inventors of those recondite beverages, cock-tail, stone-fence, and sherry cobbler."

1817 – Elizabeth Hammond publishes *Modern Domestic Cookery, and Useful Receipt Book*, which has some punch recipes.

1820 – La Piña de Plata (the Silver Pineapple) restaurant and bar opens in Havana, Cuba. No one knows what cocktails were served here at that time—yet, but one hundred years later the bar was named Bar la Florida with a nickname of Floridita. It became famous for its frozen Daiquiris and celebrity patrons including Nobel Prize winner Ernest Hemingway.
- The first blended Scotch whisky, Johnnie Walker, is produced.
- The Beefeater gin distillery is built in England.

1821 – Author James Fenimore Cooper writes about a fictional character named Betty Flanagan who invented the cock-tail. The Flanagan character was supposedly based on a real person named Catherine Hustler (1767–1832) who ran Hustler's Tavern in Lewiston, New York, during the War of 1812 and put rooster tail feathers in drinks (cock-tails).

1823 – Pimm's Cup No. 1 is first produced by James Pimm in London.
- The Gin-Twist (gin, hot water, lemon juice, and sugar) is mentioned in the novel *Saint Ronan's Well* by Sir Walter Scott.
- Bourbon County, Kentucky, starts to call their whiskey "bourbon."

1824 – George Smith founds the Glenlivet distillery.

1825 – The first lavish London gin palaces begin to be built. They are decorated with opulent style. Later, in 1836, Charles Dickens said, "perfectly dazzling when contrasted with the darkness and dirt we have just left."
- Sandeman Port is produced.

1827 – Students of Oxford University publish the first known alcoholic drink recipe book, *Oxford Night Caps: A Collection of Receipts for Making Various Beverages at the University*. Basically, college students are credited for taking the time to put together a book of recipes so they can party. They publish several editions for almost one hundred years.
- Ballantine's blended Scotch is produced.

1830 – Talisker Scotch and Tanqueray gin are produced.

1843 — Charles Dickens writes in *Martin Chuzzlewit*, "He could...smoke more tobacco, drink more rum-toddy, mint-julep, gin-sling, and cocktail, than any private gentleman of his acquaintance."
— Courvoisier Cognac is produced.
— The Tom & Jerry hot cocktail is mentioned in the *Symbol and Odd Fellow's Magazine*.

1844 — Dry vermouth produced by the Noilly Company is first introduced in America via New Orleans.

1846 — Dewar's blended Scotch whisky is established.
— Aalborg akvavit is produced in Norway.

1850 — The first known published illustration of a two-piece cocktail shaker is seen in the *London News*.

1851 — Walter and Alfred Gilbey open Gilbey's Gin Distillery.

New Orleans in 1851. New Orleans has created more cocktails than any city in the world and some served during this time include Roffignac, Sazerac, and Brandy Crusta. Other adopted popular cocktails served include Mint Julep, Old-Fashioned, and Milk Punch. For the wealthy, ice from frozen lake and ponds was also available. © *Everett Historical / Shutterstock*

1852 — Joseph Santini invents the Brandy Crusta in New Orleans.

1853 — New York barkeep George Sala talks about barkeeps in Charles Dickens's weekly twenty-four-page journal, *Household Words*. The article describes the barkeep and his assistants as scholarly gentlemen, accomplished artists, skilled acrobats, master magicians, and bottle conjurers as they throw glasses and toss bottles about.

1854 — Canadian Club whisky is produced.

1856 — The word "mixologist" is first coined in the *Knickerbocker* or *New York Monthly Magazine*.
— The London *Weekly Dispatch* quotes the *New York Times* saying, "Every sentence a man utters must be moistened with a julep or cobbler. All the affairs of life are begun and ended with drinks."

1858 – Seagram's VO whisky is produced.

1859 – American bartender Jerry Thomas begins working on his first book, which is published in 1862.

1860 – Campari is introduced by Gaspare Campari.

1862 – Jerry Thomas publishes the first known American cocktail recipe book, *Bar-Tender's Guide, How to Mix Drinks, or the Bon-Vivant's Companion.*

– The London *Weekly Dispatch* quotes the *New York Times* saying, "Every sentence a man utters must be moistened with a julep or cobbler. All the affairs of life are begun and ended with drinks."

1863 – G. E. Roberts publishes *Cups and Their Customs.*

1864 – George Pullman designs railway sleeping cars, dining cars, and lounge cars serving cocktails.

1865 – Alexander Walker, Johnnie Walker's son, develops Old Highland blended Scotch whisky.

1867 – Scotsman Lauchlin Rose introduces sweetened lime juice and names it Rose's Lime Cordial. By 1879, he perfected the packaging.

– George Dickel builds his distillery.

– *Harper's New Monthly* November issue reports that 500 bottles of sherry were opened—in one day—to make Sherry Cobblers priced at one franc at the Exposition Universelle in France. One French franc is equivalent to $13 in 2018 currency.

1868 – Articles on American cocktails and cocktail shakers are published in two British publications: the British periodical *Notes and Queries* and *Meliora: A Quarterly Review of Social Science.*

1869 – Englishman William Terrington publishes *Cooling Cups and Dainty Drinks: Collection of Recipes for "Cups" and Other Compound Drinks and of General Information on Beverages of All Kind.* He goes on to publish a second edition in 1872.

– J. Haney publishes *Haney's Steward and Barkeepers Manual.*

– Mark Twain mentions a Champagne Cocktail in his memoir *Innocents Abroad.*

– American composer Joseph Winner wrote the drinking song "Little Brown Jug." It mentions the spirits gin and rum. Seventy years later, bandleader Glenn Miller recorded it with his swing orchestra.

1872 – Lillet is produced.

1873   – At the World's Exposition held in Vienna, Austria, the American Exhibition has a giant wigwam with Native American bartenders making cocktails behind three circular bars. The Exposition's Rotunda bar introduces something new in their cocktails—straws.

1874   – The Criterion restaurant and theater open in London with an American Bar. The decor consists of mirrors and white marble.
     – Fundador Spanish brandy is produced.
     – While in the UK, Mark Twain writes a letter to his wife, Livy, to gather four ingredients for his return: Scotch whisky, Angostura bitters, lemons, and crushed sugar. He has been drinking this cocktail before breakfast, dinner, and bed at the suggestion of a surgeon to help digestion.

1875   – H. L. W publishes *American Bar-Tender* or *The Art and Mystery of Making Drinks*.
     – The Jack Daniel's Distillery is established.

1878   – L. Engel publishes *American and Other Drinks*.

1879   – O. H. Byron publishes *The Modern Bartender's Guide*.
     – J. Kirtion publishes *Intoxicating Drinks: Their History and Mystery*.
     – The Grand Hotel Stockholm opens an American Bar.
     – Myers's Dark rum is produced.

1880s   – The Cocktail à la Louisiane restaurant invents the Cocktail à la Louisiane in New Orleans.

1882   – Harry Johnson publishes *Harry Johnson's Bartender Manual* or *How to Mix Drinks of the Present Style*.
     – The first known mention of a Manhattan cocktail appears in the *Sunday Morning Herald* from Olean, New York.

1884   – E. J. Hauck patents a three-piece cocktail shaker.
     – The New York G. Winter Brewing Company publishes a list of glassware for first-rate saloons. The bartender guide lists over twenty-five types of glassware needed.

1887   – Jerry Thomas publishes the second edition of *The Bar-Tender's Guide* or *How to Mix All Kinds of Plain and Fancy Drinks*.
     – C. Paul publishes *American Drinks*.

1888   – Henry Charles "Carl" Ramos invents the Ramos Gin Fizz in New Orleans.
     – H. Lamore publishes *The Bartender* or *How to Mix Drinks*.

1890s   – Jules Alciatore invents the Café Brûlot Diabolique (Devilishly Burned Coffee) in New Orleans.

1891 – Henry J. Wehmann publishes *Wehmann's Bartenders Guide*. To date, this book has the second known reference to a Martini recipe.

– William T. Boothby publishes *Cocktail Boothby's American Bartender*.

1892 – "The Only William" Schmidt publishes *The Flowing Bowl—What and When to Drink*. Four years later, he published his second book, *Fancy Drinks and Popular Beverages*. Schmidt's books were different from all other cocktail celebrity books at the time because his recipes called for unusual items such as tonic phosphate, Calisaya (Italian herbal liqueur), crème de roses, and even a garnish that involved stenciling on a nutmeg. He had Christmas cocktails published in the paper, created a $5 cocktail ($140 in 2018 currency), and although not 100 percent confirmed—but highly believed—he was the first known gay celebrity bartender.

– George Kappeler invents the Widow's Kiss at the Holland House Hotel in New York.

– G. F. Heublein produces the first commercial Manhattan and Martini bottled cocktails, with the tagline "A better cocktail at home than is served over any bar in the world."

– Cornelius Dungan patents the double cone jigger.

1895 – C. F. Lawlor publishes *The Mixicologist* or *How to Mix All Kinds of Fancy Drinks*.

– Jack Daniel's begins bottling in its famous square bottle.

– R. C. Miller publishes *American Bar Tender*.

– George J. Kappler publishes *Modern American Drinks: How to Mix and Serve all Kinds of Cups and Drinks*.

1897 – The Rob Roy is introduced at New York's Fifth Avenue Hotel.

– Sir Thomas Dewar and Fredric Glassup release a Dewar's Scotch commercial film in New York City that is projected on a canvas screen in Herald Square at 1321 Broadway. It is the first alcohol commercial to appear on film.

1898 – The Savoy Hotel in London opens an American Bar.

– The Ward 8 cocktail is invented in Boston.

1899 – Sweden opens their first American Bar.

1900S–2000S

The Waldorf-Astoria in New York City had been open for seven years and set the standard for quality cocktails around the world. Drink making was appreciated and bartending was an art form. The hotel bar never published a cocktail book, but newspaperman and barfly Albert Crockett published *The Old Waldorf-Astoria Bar Book* in 1931 and 1935, which gives us a glimpse into that era. In the early 1900s, breweries owned most saloons, barkeeps made $15 a week ($400 in 2018 currency), and Sunday was the busiest day of the week. On January 16, 1920, the American Prohibition started, then ended December 5, 1933. The stock market crashed, media popularized cocktails, many brands were produced, discotheques increased sales, the drinking age changed twice, the AIDS epidemic hit, the stock market crashed again, and strict drinking and driving laws confused imbibers for several years—as a result of all this upheaval, the quality of cocktails sunk to an all-time low.

1912 Vintage postcard depicting the Hotel Astoria in Times Square. This hotel set the standard for cocktails around the world.
© *Susan Law Cain / Shutterstock*

There were also five significant wars in the 1900s that affected imbibing Americans: World War I, World War II, Korean War, Vietnam War, and the Gulf War. The millennium brought the skankification of women in rap music videos, the increase of Cognac sales, half-dressed female bartenders dancing on bar tops, the Cosmopolitan and the Mojito became the most popular cocktails in the world, embarrassing Martini bars popped up—but—the most important development is that the cocktail culture renaissance seeds were planted.

More technology happened during this time than 10,000 years combined. Some inventions in this century include electricity, the blender, the juicer, refrigeration, air-conditioning, the phonograph, radio, the eight-track player, the cassette tape, the compact disc, the boom box, the Walkman, DVDs, iTunes, the automobile, the airplane, the helicopter, the spaceship, motion picture theaters, talkies, drive-in theaters, television, VCRs, special-effects blockbusters, DVRs, online television, the camera, the video camera, neon lights, the zipper, stainless steel, canned beer, the telephone, the cellular phone, the smartphone, texting, the microwave, the calculator, robots, the ballpoint pen, medical discoveries, the fax machine, the pager, the computer, the internet, Skype, the Hubble space telescope, and social media.

Names of bars, saloons, and clubs in the 1900s–2000s include Fox and Hound, Filthy McNasty's, Fuzz & Firkin, Slug and Lettuce, Snooty Fox, Ciro's, Chez Victor, the Ohio Club, the Ritz, Whiskey A Go-Go, Stork Club, the Tiki Lounge, VooDoo Lounge, the Palace Saloon, Sloppy Joe's, Studio 54, Le Freak, Disco Inferno, Cabaret, Electric Cowboy, the Rainbow Room, the Starlight Room, the Velvet Tango Room, Coyote Ugly, Angel's Share, Absinthe Brassiere & Bar, and Milk & Honey, PDT, Death & Co, Honeycut, Clover Club, Bourbon & Branch, Canon, Revel, Employees Only, the Violet Room, Three Dots and a Dash, and the Dead Rabbit.

Drinking words heard include "acting like a fool," "baked," "bashed," "blasted," "blitzed," "blown away," "bombed," "bonkers," "buzzed," "canned," "creamed," "crocked," "done," "double vision," "fried," "gone," "hammered," "high," "liquored up," "lit," "party animal," "three sheets to the wind," "shitfaced," "slave to drink," "stoned," "tipsy," "toasted," and "wasted."

Brands and spirits launched in the 1900s–2000s are too many to mention, but include Cutty Sark Scotch, Havana Club rum, Jägermeister, Kahlúa, B&B, Crown Royal, Don Julio tequila, Captain Morgan spiced rum, Irish Mist, Yukon Jack, Finlandia vodka, Stoli vodka, Midori melon liqueur, Baileys Irish cream, Zacapa rum, Absolut vodka, Chambord, Peachtree schnapps, Bartles & Jaymes wine coolers, Absolut Peppar, Absolut Citron, Bombay Sapphire, Gentleman Jack, Patrón Tequila, Guinness in cans, Johnnie Walker gold, Crown Royal Reserve, Skyy vodka, Wild Turkey Rare Breed, Grey Goose vodka, Belvedere vodka, Tito's vodka, Redrum, Plymouth gin, Three Olives vodka, Smirnoff Ice, Van Gogh gin, Hendrick's gin, Jack Daniel's Single Barrel, Bulleit Bourbon, and Smirnoff flavored vodkas, Ancho Reyes Chile liqueur, Ford's gin, Chambord vodka, Zucca Amaro, St. Germain Elderflower Liqueur, Stiggins Plantation pineapple rum, and Sipsmith gin.

Early 1900s	– The Pisco Sour is invented in Peru.
1900	– Harry Johnson publishes *Harry Johnson's Bartenders' Manual or How to Mix Drinks of the Present Style*.
	– William T. Boothby publishes the second edition of *Cocktail Boothby's American Bartender*.
1902	– Louis Eppinger invented the Bamboo Cocktail in Yokohama, Japan.

1903 – Edward Spencer publishes *The Flowing Bowl*.
  – Tim Daly publishes *Daly's Bartenders' Encyclopedia*.

1904 – Frederick J. Drake and Company publishes a vest-pocket recipe book, *Drinks as They Are Mixed*. The recipes were gathered by leading Chicago bartenders.
  – John Applegreen publishes *Applegreen's Bar Book*. This book contains a recipe for a Martini Cocktail.
  – Paris Ritz bartender Frank P. Newman publishes *American-Bar Recettes des Boissons Anglaises et Américaine*.

1905 – Johnnie Solon invents the Bronx cocktail at the Waldorf-Astoria Hotel.
  – Charles S. Mahoney publishes *The Hoffman House Bartender's Guide*.

1906 – Louis Muckensturm publishes *Louis' Mixed Drinks*. This is the first book in English calling for gin and vermouth for the Dry Martini recipe.
  – George J. Kappeler publishes *Modern American Drinks: How to Mix and Serve All Kinds of Cups and Drinks*.

1908 – Hon. Wm. Boothby publishes *The World's Drinks and How to Mix Them Standard Authority*.

1910 – First in-flight cocktails are served to paying passengers on a scheduled airliner, on the Zeppelin flying over Germany.

1911 – Sir Thomas Dewar erects the world's largest mechanical sign (sixty-eight feet) advertising Dewar's Scotch whisky on the Thames River embankment.

1912 – Charles S. Mahoney publishes *The Hoffman House Bartender's Guide*.
  – The Bartenders Association of America publishes *Bartenders' Manual*.

1914 – Jacques Straub publishes *Drinks*.

1915 – The El Presidente cocktail is invented at Bar la Florida (Floridita) in Havana, Cuba.

1916 – The first recorded cocktail party is hosted by Mrs. Julius S. Walsh Jr. from St. Louis, Missouri, and published in the *St. Paul Pioneer Press* newspaper mentioning cocktails: Clover Leafs, Highballs, Gin Fizzes, Bronxes, Martinis, and Manhattans.
  – Hugo R. Ensslin publishes *Recipes for Mixed Drinks*. The book mentions the first Aviation cocktail.

1917 – Even though African Americans had been tending bar since the 1700s, Tom Bullock is the first to publish a cocktail recipe book, *The Ideal Bartender*.

1919
- Harry MacElhone publishes *Harry's ABC of Mixing Cocktails*. One of the most popular cocktails is the White Lady.
- American tourists love Italy's Torino-Milano cocktail, so the name was changed to Americano.
- The Grasshopper is believed to be invented at Tujague's in New Orleans.

1920
- Americans flock to Cuba, Mexico, and Canada to drink legal cocktails.
- Bertha E. L. Stockbridge publishes *What to Drink*.
- The book *This Side of Paradise* by F. Scott Fitzgerald has the first known literary mention of the Daiquiri.

1922
- Patrick McGarry invents the Buck's Fizz at the Buck's Club in London.
- Harry MacElhone invents the Brandy Alexander at Ciro's in London.
- The Blood and Sand cocktail is created after Rudolph Valentino from the film of the same name.
- It is believed that Fosco Scarselli creates the Negroni.

1923
- Harry MacElhone invents the Monkey Gland at the New York Bar in Paris.
- Bartender Frank Meier invents the Mimosa at the Ritz Hotel in Paris, France

1924
- Harry MacElhone and O. O. McIntyre create the International Bar Flies at the New York Bar in Paris.

1927
- Harry MacElhone publishes *Barflies and Cocktails* in Paris.

1928
- Jerry Thomas's book is republished (Thomas died in 1885) with the title *The Bon Vivants Companion or How to Mix Drinks*.

1930
- Harry Craddock publishes *Savoy Cocktail Book*.
- Greta Garbo stars in her first "talkie," *Anna Christie*, and her first words are "Gimme a whiskey, ginger ale on the side."

1932
- The Napier Company produces a cocktail shaker with engraved recipes called the Tells-You-How Mixer.
- Davide Campari packages Campari and soda water in cone-shaped bottles.

1934
- Walter Bergeron invents the Vieux Carré cocktail at the Carousel Bar in New Orleans.
- Don the Beachcomber invents the Zombie in Hollywood, California.

- The first *Thin Man* film is released starring William Powell and Myrna Loy. Cocktails seen include Martini, Bronx, and Knickerbocker. Powell says his famous line when showing the bartenders how to shake a cocktail: "The important thing is the rhythm. Always have rhythm in your shaking. Now, a Manhattan you shake to foxtrot time; a Bronx, to two-step time; a dry Martini you always shake to waltz time."
- Jazz Bandleader and singer Cab Calloway releases the song "The Call of the Jitterbug." The first line of the song is "If you'd like to be a jitterbug, first thing you must do is get a jug, put whiskey, wine, and gin within and shake it all up and then begin."

Jazz singer, songwriter, and bandleader Cab Calloway. © *Photofest*

1936
- The Bacardi Cocktail is the first and only cocktail to date to win a court case making it illegal to serve this cocktail without using Bacardi rum.
- Kahlúa Mexican coffee liqueur is introduced.

1937
- Constantino Ribaliagua Vert invents the Hemingway Special (Papa Dobl) at Bar la Florida (Floridita) in Havana, Cuba.

1939
- The Zombie is served at the 1939 New York World's Fair.
- Crown Royal is introduced. It was created for Queen Elizabeth's visit to Canada.

1940s
- The Moscow Mule is invented.

1942
- Pat O'Brien invents the Hurricane in New Orleans.
- Joseph Sheridan invents the Irish Coffee at Foynes Airbase in Limerick, Ireland.
- It is believed that the Rusty Nail is invented in Hawaii.
- The film *Casablanca* is popular and many cocktails are seen in Rick's Bar.

1944
- Trader Vic invents the Mai Tai in Oakland, California.

1945
- The Andrews Sisters release the song "Rum and Coca-Cola" and it becomes the #1 song in America. Radio stations ban the song, which makes it even more popular.
- Giuseppe Cipriani invents the Bellini at Harry's Bar in Venice, Italy, but does not name it until 1948.
- Victor Bergeron publishes *Trader Vic's Bartender's Guide*.

1948
- The Margarita becomes the official drink of Mexico.
- A small group of California bartenders—who were overseas members of the United Kingdom Bartenders' Guild—start a California branch of that organization in the Los Angeles area.
- Gustave Tops invents the Black Russian at the Hotel Metropole in Brussels.
- The first known mention of a cocktail on a radio show is heard. Guests at a party order Stingers from the butler on *The Whistler* radio drama show, "Guilty Conscience". Several references are made to their intoxicating strength.

1952
- Stanton Delaplane brings the Irish Coffee to the Buena Vista Cafe in San Francisco. Today they sell over 2,000 a day.

1953
- Ian Fleming writes about a fictional character named James Bond. In chapter seven, Bond orders a Dry Martini served in a deep champagne goblet with three measures of Gordon's gin, one of Gordon's vodka, and half a measure of Lillet dry vermouth, then shaken very well until ice-cold, and topped with a garnish of lemon peel. This is the first reference to combining both vodka and gin in a Martini. It is named Vesper.

1954
- The Piña Colada is invented at the Caribe Hilton's Beachcomber Bar in San Juan, Puerto Rico.

1955
- The Rat Pack, headed by Frank Sinatra, glamorizes cocktails by holding them on stage and during TV performances.

Singer and actor Frank Sinatra on the 1950s. © *Photofest*

1957 – Harry Yee invents the Blue Hawaii at the Hawaiian Village on the Island of O'ahu.

1957 – The Piña Colada becomes Puerto Rico's official drink by winning a global award.

1951 – The International Bartenders Association (IBA) is started.

1960 – The first Playboy Club opens at 116 East Walton in Chicago and becomes the busiest bar in the world, often serving 1,400 guests a day. Cocktails cost $1.50 ($13 in 2018 currency).

1962 – The first James Bond film, *Dr. No*, shows Sean Connery making a Smirnoff Martini in his hotel room and ordering Vodka Martinis shaken not stirred. In today's terminology—it went viral.

1965 – Alan Stillman opens a New York City bar and grill as the first public cocktail party hang and names it TGI Friday's (Thank God It's Friday). *Lifetime* magazine credited Friday's with ushering in the Singles Era and within six months of opening, Stillman was written up in *Time*, *Newsweek*, and the *Saturday Evening Post*. Before then, there was not a place for twenty- and thirty-somethings to meet except for cocktail parties held around the city in homes and apartments. Stillman painted the building blue, put up red-and-white-striped awnings, bought the staff red-and-white-striped shirts, threw sawdust on the floor, hung up some Tiffany lamps, and added brass railings. Many creative, fun, and party cocktails were birthed in TGI Friday's.

1966 – India's ambassador B. N. Chakravarty says, "Americans are a funny lot. They drink whiskey to keep warm; then they put some ice in to make it cool. They put sugar in to make it sweet; and then they put a slice of lemon in it to make it sour. Then they say, 'Here's to you' and drink it themselves."

1969 – Bobby Lozoff invents the Tequila Sunrise in Sausalito, California, while tending bar at The Trident.

1972 – Robert "Rosebud" Butt in Long Island, New York, invents the Long Island Iced Tea while tending bar at Oak Beach Inn.

– Stolichnaya vodka is introduced.

– The TV show *M*A*S*H* debuts. The lead doctor characters, Hawkeye and Trapper John, drink Martinis from the still they built in their quarters.

1973 – After the Vietnam War, TGI Friday's begins franchising all over the world and actually stays a fresh bar until the late 1970s. TGI Friday's set a standard when it came to training staff. They had a reputation for the most challenging training programs for any chain restaurant/ bar in the world. They created the first bartender gods since the beginning of Prohibition. TGI Friday's bartenders also started flair bartending, which led to the 1988 Tom Cruise film *Cocktail*.

– Jose Cuervo puts the recipe for a Tequila Sunrise on the back of their bottle, then three months later the Eagles release their hit song "Tequila Sunrise."

1974 – Baileys Irish cream is introduced and new drinks created include the Mississippi Mudslide and B-52.

1975 – In the fall, Neal Murray creates the first known Cosmopolitan.

1977 – Jimmy Buffett releases the song "Margaritaville," making the Margarita the most popular drink of the year—and it has stayed in the top ten since.

– Stan Jones publishes the Jones' Complete Barguide.

– The first known newspaper mention of a Kamikaze was in the February 1 issue of the Minneapolis Star.

1978 – Midori melon liqueur is launched to create the Melon Ball for the wrap party of *Saturday Night Fever* at Studio 54. Midori Sours become popular.

1979 – The Piña Colada is popular due to Rupert Holmes's Piña Colada song, "Escape."

– Absolut vodka is introduced.

– Ray Foley publishes *Bartender Magazine*.

1981 – Neal Murray (1975 inventor of the Cosmopolitan) introduces San Francisco to the Cosmopolitan at the Elite Café (2049 Fillmore Street).

1982 – Schumann's Cocktail Bar opens in Munich, Germany.

1984
- Peachtree schnapps and Captain Morgan spiced rum are introduced.
- The Fuzzy Navel becomes popular.
- Earl Bernhardt and Pam Fortner invent the Hand Grenade® for the 1984 Louisiana World Exposition.
- The Sex on the Beach cocktail becomes popular.

1985
- General Manager of the Fog City Diner in San Francisco, Doug "Bix" Biederbeck, hires Neal Murray as a bartender where he makes his Cosmopolitan making the cocktail even more popular.
- Balladeer and researcher Tayler Vrooman was fascinated with songs from the 1600s and 1700s and released his album *Baroque Bacchanalian*. On the album, there are songs about drinking with titles that include "Come Let Us Drink About," "Good Claret," "The Delights of the Bottle," and "The Thirsty Toper."

1986
- Chef Paul Prudhomme invents the Cajun Martini in New Orleans.
- TGI Friday's makes a bartender video of company bartenders John "JB" Bandy, John Mescall, and "Magic" Mike Werner. Later in the year, the company holds the first flair bartending competition in Woodland Hills, California, and calls it Bar Olympics. John "JB" Bandy wins.
- Absolut launches their first flavored vodka, Absolut Peppar.

1987
- After Touchstone Productions interviews thirty-four bartenders, they chose John "JB" Bandy to be the flair instructor for Tom Cruise and Bryan Brown for the 1988 film *Cocktail*.
- In October, bartender Patrick "Paddy" Mitten brings the Cosmopolitan cocktail to New York City from San Francisco and begins serving it at the Life Café (343 E 10th Street B).

The first flair bartending video (VHS) in 1989 by the first flair bartending competition winner, John "JB" Bandy. JB taught Tom Cruise and Bryan Brown flair bartending for the 1988 film *Cocktail*. © John "JB" Bandy

1988
- *Cocktail*, the film starring Tom Cruise as a bartender, ignites flair bartending around the world.
- Absolut Citron, Bombay Sapphire, Gentleman Jack, and Guinness in cans are introduced.

- Dale "King Cocktail" DeGroff begins a gourmet approach to cocktails at the Rainbow Room in New York City.

1989
- Unaware of any other cocktail called a Cosmopolitan, Cheryl Cook creates her Cosmopolitan in March 1989.
- Kathy Casey from Seattle, Washington, pioneers the bar chef movement.
- The world's longest bar is installed at the Beer Barrel Saloon in South Bass Island, Ohio.
- The bar has 160 barstools and is 405' and 10" long (that's 45' and 10" longer than a football field).
- Melissa Huffsmith brings the Cosmopolitan cocktail to The Odeon from the Life Cafe (New York City). With a selection of higher quality ingredients to choose from she revamps the Cosmopolitan cocktail using Absolut Citron, Cointreau, fresh lime juice, and cranberry.

1990
- The first Portland, Oregon, fresh classic bar, Zefiro, opens.

1991
- Gary Regan publishes *The Bartender's Bible*.
- Wild Turkey Rare Breed is introduced.
- Charles Schumann publishes Schumann's American Bar Book.

1992
- Cocktail godfather Paul Harrington is recognized in San Francisco for making classic cocktails.
- Absolut Kurrant, Johnnie Walker Gold, and Crown Royal Reserve are introduced.

1993
- The first known cocktail recipe book to list the Cosmopolitan cocktail is *The Complete Book of Mixed Drinks* by Anthony Dias Blue. Blue credits Julie's Supper Club in San Francisco for the recipe.
- *Straight Up or On the Rocks* is published by William Grimes.

1994
- Scotland celebrates 500 years of whisky production.
- On Wednesday, November 16 in *The Central New Jersey Home News* (New Brunswick, New Jersey) the first known recipe for a Cosmopolitan is published in a newspaper. The recipe was contributed by Dale DeGroff.

1995
- The first World Wide Web cocktail-related sites are launched: barmedia.com, bartender.com, cocktail.com (defunct), cocktailtime.com (defunct), martiniplace.com (defunct), and webtender.com.
- Bacardi Limon rum is introduced.
- Steve Olson begins teaching "Gin Cocktail Clinics" helping consumers make fresh and classic cocktails in their homes.

1996 – Sammy Hagar's Cabo Wabo Tequila and the first organic vodka, Rain, are introduced.

– Paulius Nasvytis opens the classic cocktail bar the Velvet Tango Room in Cleveland, Ohio.

– The Corona Limona becomes popular (a shot of Bacardi Limon rum in a Corona beer).

– The film *Swingers* shows characters drinking classic cocktails and quality booze, which helps set the tone for the germinating craft cocktail movement.

1997 – *Quench*, on the Food Network, brings cocktails to TV.

– Simon Difford's Class Magazine is launched.

– Grey Goose vodka and Chopin vodka are introduced.

– Jared Brown and Anistatia Miller publish *Shaken Not Stirred: A Celebration of the Martini*.

– Gary Regan publishes *New Classic Cocktails*.

Paul Harrington and Laura Moorhead, authors of the ground-breaking 1998 cocktail book, *Cocktail: The Drinks Bible for the 21st Century*. © *Paul Harrington*

1998 – Paul Harrington and Laura Moorhead publish the game-changing *Cocktail: The Drinks Bible for the 21st Century*.

– On April 9, the first known Cosmopolitan cocktail seen and mentioned on a television show was written into the show *ER* by Linda Gase. The season 4 episode 17 is called "A Bloody Mess."

– Patrick Sullivan opens B-Side Lounge, which is considered Boston's first fresh classic cocktail bar.

– Tony Abou-Ganim is hired to bring classic fresh cocktails to all twenty-three bars at Bellagio in Las Vegas.

– The first known videogame to mention a cocktail is Metal Gear Solid when Nastasha Romanenko says that a Stinger is her favorite cocktail.

- On July 19, season one, episode seven "The Monogamists," the Cosmopolitan cocktail was first mentioned on the HBO show *Sex and the City*. The voice-over of the character Carrie Bradshaw read: "That afternoon I dragged my poor, tortured soul out to lunch with Stanford Blach and attempted to stun it senseless with Cosmopolitans.

1999 - Smirnoff Ice, Absolut Mandarin, Van Gogh gin, Hendrick's gin, and Jack Daniel's Single Barrel are introduced.
- Tommy's Mexican Restaurant in San Francisco becomes the number-one tequila bar in America.
- David Wondrich begins to update the online version of Esquire's 1949 *Handbook for Hosts*.
- Ted A. Breaux becomes the first to analyze vintage absinthe using modern science, the results sparking a paradigm shift in our understanding of the infamous spirit.
- Sasha Petraske opens Milk & Honey on New Year's Eve in New York City.
- In the second season of the HBO TV show *Sex and the City*, the Cosmopolitan becomes the new worldwide hottest cocktail due to being seen in ten episodes and verbally mentioned in three episodes. It pairs nicely with the flavored Martini craze and Martini bars found in all major cities that offered 200+ flavored Martinis on their menus.

2000 - The film *Coyote Ugly* shows scantily clad cowgirl bartenders slinging whiskey and dancing on the bar top.
- Tanqueray 10, Alizé, Tequiza, Smirnoff Twist flavored vodkas, and Wild Turkey Russell's Reserve are introduced.
- The Beekman Arms of Rhinebeck in New York is the oldest continuously operating tavern in America.

2001 - Hpnotiq plans to launch on September 11, but America is attacked, so the launch takes place months later.
- Gary Regan begins conducting a series of two-day bartender workshops called Cocktails in the Country.

2002 - After forty years, James Bond makes another cocktail popular around the world. Pierce Brosnan (Bond) holds a Mojito in Cuba and then hands it to orange bikini–clad Halle Berry—overnight, it revives the classic Mojito and is still one of the most ordered cocktails in the world today. Bartenders are bombarded with drink requests and 99 percent of them do not have one mint leaf behind the bar.

- Dekuyper Sour Apple Pucker is introduced.
- Dale "King Cocktail" DeGroff publishes the book that officially kicks off the craft cocktail movement, *The Craft of the Cocktail: Everything You Need to Know to Be a Master Bartender*.
- The Appletini becomes popular.
- The first cocktail festival, Tales of the Cocktail is launched in New Orleans.
- William Grimes publishes Straight Up or On the Rocks: The Story of the American Cocktail.
- Jeff "Beachbum" Berry publishes *Intoxica*.
- Kevin Brauch hosts the drinking travel series TV show *The Thirsty Traveler*.
- The first known film to show and mention a Cosmopolitan cocktail is *Juwanna Mann*.

Country music star Alan Jackson in 2003. © *Photofest*

2003
- Julie Reiner opens Flatiron Lounge, the first high-volume craft cocktail bar in New York City.
- Colin Peter Field publishes *The Cocktails of Ritz Paris.*
- Alan Jackson and Jimmy Buffett release the song "It's Five O'clock Somewhere."

2004
- The Museum of the American Cocktail is founded in New Orleans by Dale and Jill DeGroff, Chris and Laura McMillian, Ted Haigh, Robert Hess, Phil Greene, and Jared Brown and Anistatia Miller.
- Absolut Raspberri is introduced.
- Ted Haigh publishes Vintage Spirits and Forgotten Cocktails.
- The award-winning bar Employees Only opens in New York City.
- Jeff "Beachbum" Berry publishes *Taboo Table*.

2005
- Sasha Petraske opens Little Branch in New York City.
- Captain Morgan Tattoo, Absolut Peach, Starbuck's coffee liqueur, Barsol pisco, Cognac Toulouse-Lautrec XO, Baileys Caramel, Baileys Chocolate Mint, and NAVAN are introduced.

- In September, University of Pennsylvania archaeochemist Patrick McGovern announces the discovery of 5,000-year-old Mesopotamian earthenware from the banks of the Tigris between Iran and Iraq that contain traces of honey, barley, tartaric acid, and apple juice. McGovern described this cocktail as "grog."
- Audrey Saunders opens Pegu Club in New York City.
- Heavy Water vodka from Anistatia Miller and Jared Brown is introduced.
- David Wondrich publishes *Killer Cocktails*.

2006
- CMT airs a reality show called *Inside the Real Coyote Ugly*. Ten women are chosen out of one thousand to learn how to bartend *Coyote Ugly*-style.
- Karen Foley publishes the award-winning drinks magazine Imbibe.
- Oprah Winfrey and Rachael Ray make a Lemon Drop Martini and a Pomegranate Martini on the Oprah Winfrey Show. Bartenders all over America are asked for these cocktails.
- The Jäger Bomb becomes popular.
- Sasha Petraske, Christy Pope, and Chad Solomon start Cuffs & Buttons—a beverage consultant and catering company.
- X-Rated Fusion, 10 Cane rum, Gran Patrón Platinum 100 percent Agave Tequila, Michael Collins Irish single malt, Rhum Clément Very Superior Old Pale (VSOP) rum, Rittenhouse 21, Skyy 90, Yamazaki 18, and Domaine Charbay Pomegranate vodka are introduced.
- Jamie Boudreau opens the craft bar Vessel in Seattle, Washington.
- Wayne Curtis publishes And a Bottle of Rum: A History of the New World in Ten Cocktails.
- Camper English pioneers "directional freezing" to make perfectly clear ice.
- San Francisco Cocktail Week starts its first year.
- Jared Brown and Anistatia Miller publish Mixologist: The Journal of the American Cocktail Vol. 1.
- Dale "King Cocktail" DeGroff, Steven Olson, Doug Frost, Paul Pacult, David Wondrich, and Andy Seymour open Beverage Alcohol Resource (BAR) in New York City.
- The bartenders of Absinthe Brassiere & Bar publish Art of the Bar.
- Dave Kaplan and Alex Day open Death + Co. on New Year's Eve in New York City.

2007 — Lucid absinthe becomes the first wormwood absinthe allowed back into the United States after being banned for ninety-five years.
— Sean Combs launches Ciroc vodka.
— Tony Abou-Ganim publishes *Modern Mixology*.
— The TV show Mad Men debuts and sparks a worldwide interest in classic cocktails.
— Jim Meehan opens PDT in New York City, and the telephone booth entrance creates headlines.
— Eric Seed brings crème de violette back into America after being unavailable for almost ninety years.
— St. Germain Elderflower Liqueur, Chivas Regal 25, Absolut New Orleans, Kubler absinthe, Appleton Estate Reserve, 360 vodka, Grey Goose Le Poire, and Tanqueray Rangspur are introduced.
— Greg Boehm begins to reproduce and publish vintage cocktail books.
— Don Lee invents fat washing by infusing bacon with Bourbon and creates the Benton's Old-Fashioned at PDT in New York City.
— Donald Trump introduces Trump vodka (and he does not drink).
— Colin Kimball launches the Small Screen Network bringing professional online bartending videos to the cocktail community.
— Derek Brown opens the first stand-alone craft cocktail bar in DC, the Gibson, with Eric Hilton, one of the founding members of Thievery Corporation.
— CeeLo Green introduces Ty Ku Sake.
— David Wondrich publishes the James Beard Award-winning *Imbibe!*
— Jared Brown and Anistatia Miller publish *Mixologist: The Journal of the American Cocktail Vol. 2*.
— Tobin Ellis is selected as the number-one bartender in America to compete against Bobby Flay in his TV show *Throwdown! with Bobby Flay*, making Ellis the first successful award-winning flair bartender to cross over to the craft cocktail world.

2008 — The Sazerac becomes the official cocktail of New Orleans through Bill No. 6.
— Julie Reiner opens Clover Club in Brooklyn, New York.
— *Indiana Jones and the Kingdom of the Crystal Skull debuts and* Dan Aykroyd introduces Crystal Head vodka which comes in a glass skull head. Coincidence?

- LXTV associated with NBC hosts a TV show sponsored by Absolut vodka titled *On the Rocks: The Search for America's Top Bartender.* The intro of the show says that there are more than 500,000 bartenders in America.
- Sasha Petraske opens White Star absinthe bar in New York City.
- Jeff "Beachbum" Berry publishes *Sippin' Safari.*
- Cocktail Kingdom is launched, selling high-quality master mixology bar tools.
- Robert Hess publishes *The Essential Bartender's Guide.*
- Prairie organic vodka, Tru2 organic gin, Compass Box Hedonism Maximus Scotch, Cape North vodka, Jett vodka, Canadian Club 30, (ri)1 Kentucky Straight rye, Maestro Dobel Diamond tequila, Siembra Azul tequila, and 1800 Silver Select tequila are introduced.
- Scott Beattie publishes *Artisanal Cocktails.*
- Bridget Albert publishes *Market Fresh Mixology.*
- Dale "King Cocktail" DeGroff publishes his second book, *The Essential Cocktail.*
- Natalie Bovis publishes the first nonalcoholic craft mocktail book, *Preggatinis: Mixology for the Mom-to-Be.*

2009
- The Ritz-Carlton launches a new global "Bar Experience" that features an edible bar menu with a fresh twist on solid and traditional cocktails.
- Sasha Petraske opens Los Angeles's first craft bar, the Varnish, with Eric Alperin. One year later, Alperin teaches actor Ryan Gosling how to make an Old-Fashioned for the 2011 film *Crazy, Stupid, Love,* which combined with the popularity of the *Mad Men* Old-Fashioned sparks a new interest for a new generation and becomes the number-one most ordered cocktail of the year.
- The Mai Tai becomes the official cocktail of Oakland, California.
- Justin Timberlake introduces 9:01 Tequila. He names it 9:01 because he says that is the time when things start happening at night.
- Absolut airs a bartender mixology TV show special called *On the Rocks.*
- Tobin Ellis starts the world's first pop-up speakeasy series called Social Mixology.
- Sasha Petraske opens Dutch Kills in Long Island City, New York.

- Dry Fly vodka, Stolichnaya Elit vodka, Charbay tequila, Evan Williams single barrel, Beefeater 24, Appleton 30, Double Cross vodka, Bluecoat gin, Vieux Carré absinthe, Bulldog gin, Citadelle Reserve, and Fruitlab organic liqueurs are introduced.
- Ted Haigh publishes the second edition of *Vintage Spirits and Forgotten Cocktails: From the Alamagoozlum to the Zombie 100 Rediscovered Recipes and the Stories Behind Them.*
- Rap star Ludacris introduces Conjure Cognac.
- On November 6—to celebrate their fifteenth anniversary—Consejo Regulador del Tequila wins a Guinness World Record for the largest display of tequila at Hospicio Cabañas, Guadalajara, Mexico. They display 1,201 bottles of tequila from all the states in Mexico.
- The chorus starts with, "Pour me somethin' tall an' strong, make it a Hurricane before I go insane." The flair bartender in the music video is Rob Husted who runs flairbar.com.
- Absolut vanilla and Blavod black vodka are introduced.
- Gary Regan publishes *The Joy of Mixology.*
- The first known song to mention a Cosmopolitan cocktail is "Cosmopolitans" written and performed by Erin McKeown.

Darcy O'Neil's award-winning 2010 book, *Fix the Pumps.*
© *Paul Mitchell*

2010
- David Wondrich publishes *Punch: The Delights (and Dangers) of the Flowing Bowl*
- Jeffrey Morgenthaler ages a barrel of Negronis and kick-starts the barrel-aged cocktail movement.
- Delta Airlines adds simple fresh cocktails on their flights.

- The owners of the award-winning New York City bar Employees Only publish *Speakeasy: The Employees Only Guide to Classic Cocktails Reimagined.* Darcy O'Neil publishes the award-winning book *Fix the Pumps.*
- Virgin America Airlines offers a few classic cocktails to passengers.

- Zane Lamprey hosts an alcohol travel show, *Three Sheets*.
- Tony Abou-Ganim publishes *The Modern Mixologist*.
- YouTuber turned Cooking Channel star—who also explores cocktails—hosts the TV show *Nadia G's Bitchin' Kitchen*.
- Chambord vodka, Zucca Amaro, Solerno blood orange liqueur, Maker's 46, Evan Williams Cherry Reserve Kentucky, ZU Zubrowka Bison Grass vodka, Ransom Old Tom gin, Glenfiddich 40, Bacardi Reserva Limitada rum, Avión tequila, Dulce Vida tequila, Eades Small Batch Speyside whisky, Conjure Cognac, Cognac Frapin Domaine Château de Fontpinot XO, Etude XO Alambic brandy, Bottega Sambuca d'Anice Stellato, Rökk vodka, and Purity vodka are introduced.
- New trends include slow cocktails (growing your own herbs at home and at the bar), barrel-aged cocktails, pre-Prohibition-style classic cocktails, cold maceration, molecular mixology, mezcal and tequila forward cocktails, punches, moonshine, genever, ginger beer, coconut water, almond milk, shrubs, honeycomb, gourmet bitters, organic products, quality vermouth, tiki bars, all types of ice, soda fountain equipment, siphons, Red Rover Bartenders (celebrity bartenders swapping/traveling to bartend at other bars), flair bartenders crossing over to mixology, spirit and cocktail classes, craft dive bars, cocktails on tap, regular bars with skilled bartenders and good drinks, food and cocktail pairings, and cocktail networking through social media.
- The Dry Martini Bar in Barcelona sells their one millionth Martini on June 30. The cocktail bar has had a giant digital counter since 1978 that has been tracking the classic Martinis made with gin or vodka.

Jamie Boudreau at Canon in Seattle, Washington.
© *Jamie Boudreau*

2011
- Ryan Gosling makes an Old-Fashioned in the film *Crazy, Stupid, Love*, which results in the cocktail being ordered more than ever.
- The cocktail competition Speed Rack is launched by Lynnette Morrero and Ivy Mix.

– On March 30, TGI Friday's in the UK celebrate their twenty-fifth anniversary by breaking a world record. They had the most people cocktail flairing simultaneously for two minutes. The event was held outdoors at the Covent Garden Piazza in London with 101 flair bartenders wearing all black-and-red-and-white-striped ties.

– Bacardi Oakheart, Angel's Envy bourbon, Johnnie Walker Double Black, Drambuie 15, St. George gin, Hakushu Japanese whisky, Pierre-Ferrand 1840, Brugal 1888, Art in the Age Rhuby, Bols Barrel-Aged Genever, Grand Marnier Quintessence, High West double rye, High West Silver OMG Pure rye, No. 3 London dry, Knob Creek single barrel, and Ron De Jeremy rum (named after the porn star) are introduced.

– Jim Meehan publishes *The PDT Cocktail Book: The Complete Bartender's Guide from the Celebrated Speakeasy*.

– Colin Peter Field publishes *Le Ritz Paris—Une Histoire de Cocktails*, which has a preface written by celebrity Kate Moss.

– On February 11, the New World Trading Company hosts the world's largest gin-tasting event with 796 participants across nine venues in London.

– Jamie Boudreau opens his award-winning bar, Canon in Seattle, Washington.

2012
– Tony Conigliaro publishes the award-winning book *Drinks*.

– Sammy Hagar introduces Sammy Hagar's Beach Bar rum.

– On July 13, Nick Nicora makes the world's largest Margarita, taking the title away from Margaritaville in Las Vegas. Nicora makes it at the California State Fair; the drink is 10,499 gallons. It is made in a large cocktail shaker and sponsored by Jose Cuervo and Cointreau.

– Ford's gin, Templeton rye, High West Whiskey Campfire, L'Essence de Courvoisier, Western Son Texas vodka, Imbue Petal & Thorn vermouth, Amsterdam gin, Leopold Brothers Fernet, and Waha.k.a. Madre Cuishe mezcal are introduced.

– Philip Greene publishes *To Have and Have Another: A Hemingway Cocktail Companion*.

2013
– Tony Conigliaro's award-winning 2012 book, *Drinks*, is reprinted and titled *The Cocktail Lab: Unveiling the Mysteries of Flavor and Aroma in Drink, with Recipes*.

– Kenny Chesney introduces Blue Chair Bay rum.

- Amy Stewart publishes the award-winning book *The Drunken Botanist.*
- Jim Beam Devil's Cut, Montelobos mezcal, Penny Blue XO rum, Art in the Age Snap, Four Roses Single Barrel 2013, Woody Creek Colorado vodka, Kirk and Sweeney rum, St. George Dry Rye Reposado gin, Papa's Pilar blonde rum, Pow-Wow botanical rye, New Columbia Distillers Green Hat Distilled gin, and George T. Stagg 2013 are introduced.
- Award-winning bartender Charles Joly introduces a line of bottled cocktails called Crafthouse Cocktails Southside.
- Jeff "Beachbum" Berry publishes *Beachbum Berry's Potions of the Caribbean.*
- George Clooney introduces Casamigos Tequila.
- Diageo hosts the world's largest cocktail-making class on September 18 in Barcelona with 1774 participants. It was run by global ambassador Kenji Jesse.
- After sixteen years, Anistatia Miller and Jared Brown publish a second edition of *Shaken Not Stirred: A Celebration of the Martini.*

Award-winning drink writers and historians Anistatia Miller and Jared Brown; 2017. © *Anistatia Miller and Jared Brown*

2014
- Kate Gerwin becomes the first winner (and first woman) to be crowned Bols Bartending World Champion.
- *Death & Co: Modern Classic Cocktails* is published by Dave Kaplan and Nick Fauchald.

- Ancho Reyes Chile liqueur, Mister Katz rock and rye, Green Spot Irish whiskey, Sapling Maple Bourbon, Roca Patrón Añejo tequila, Anchor Old Tom gin, St. George California Reserve Agricole rum, High West A Midwinter Night's Dram, A Smith Bowman Abraham Bowman Bourbon, Elijah Craig 23, and Tanqueray Old Tom gin are introduced.
- The Smithsonian TV show *The United States of Drinking* is hosted by award-winning food writer Josh Ozersky.
- Jeffrey Morgenthaler publishes *The Bar Book: Elements of Cocktail Technique.*
- The Savoy celebrates its 125th birthday on August 6.

- On April 27, the 4-Jack's Bar and Bistro in Punta Cana, Dominican Republic, makes the world's largest Mojito with the Dominican rum Punta Cana. It takes forty people one hour and thirty-five minutes and contains 185 gallons of rum.
- In March, bartender Sheldon Wiley becomes the world's fastest bartender by breaking the Guinness World Record for making the most cocktails in one hour. It is sponsored by Stoli vodka and the official rules are: each cocktail requires a minimum of three ingredients and no cocktail can be duplicated. He makes 1905 cocktails. The event is held at New York's Bounce Sporting Club.

2015
- Salvatore "The Maestro" Calabrese publishes a second edition of *Classic Cocktails*.
- *Cocktails & Classics* is hosted by Michael Urie and celebrity friends who watch and critique classic films while sipping cocktails.
- David Wondrich publishes the second edition of *Imbibe! Updated and Revised Edition: From Absinthe Cocktail to Whiskey Smash, a Salute in Stories and Drinks to "Professor" Jerry Thomas, Pioneer of the American Bar.*
- Crown Royal rye, Amaro di Angostura, La Caravedo pisco, Tanqueray Bloomsbury, Cynar 70, Encanto pisco, Rieger & Co. Midwestern Dry gin, Rieger & Co. Kansas City whiskey, Highspire pure rye, Grey Goose VX, Sipsmith gin, Redemption Rye Barrel Proof, Stiggins Plantation pineapple rum, Fernet Francisco, Caña Brava rum, Balsam American Amaro, Mr. Lyan Bottled Cocktails, Bacardi tangerine rum, Portobello gin, and Small Hand Foods Yeoman tonic syrups are introduced.
- The owners of the award-winning New York City bar Dead Rabbit publish *The Dead Rabbit Drinks Manual: Secret Recipes and Barroom Tales from Two Belfast Boys Who Conquered the Cocktail World.*
- Philip Greene publishes an updated version of *To Have and Have Another: A Hemingway Cocktail Companion.*
- Chris McMillian and his wife, Laura open their first bar, Revel Café & Bar in New Orleans.

2016
- Jamie Boudreau, owner of the award-winning Seattle bar Canon, publishes *The Canon Cocktail Book: Recipes from the Award-Winning Bar.*
- Chris McMillian and Elizabeth M. Williams publish *Lift Your Spirits: A Celebratory History of Cocktail Culture in New Orleans.*

- Jack Daniel's 150th Anniversary; Three Olives pink grapefruit, pineapple, and pear vodka; Cockspur old gold rum; Life of Reilley Disco Lemonade; Clayton Bourbon; Bird Dog chocolate whiskey; Old Home maple whiskey; Don Q 151 rum; Jameson Cooper's Croze; Mount Gay XO; Brooklyn gin; Crown Royal honey; Yukon Jack Wicked Hot; E. J. peach brandy; Pau Maui pineapple vodka; Uncle Bob's root beer whiskey, Laphroig 15, and Jack Daniel's Single Barrel rye are introduced.
- Robert Simonson publishes *A Proper Drink.*
- Owners of the award-winning San Francisco bar Smuggler's Cove, Martin and Rebecca Cate, publish *Smuggler's Cove: Exotic Cocktails, Rum, and the Cult of Tiki.*
- Billy Gibbons from the band ZZ Top introduces Pura Vida tequila.
- Sasha Petraske's *Regarding Cocktails* is published by his widow, Georgette.

2017
- Laird's 12-Year-Old Rare Apple Brandy, Hendrick's Orbium Gin, Slow & Low Rock & Rye Canned Old Fashioned, La Gritona Reposado Tequila, Two James Doctor Bird Jamaican Rum, Santo Mezquila Tequila, and Mr. Black Coffee Amaro are released.
- Actor George Clooney sells Casamigos Tequila to Diageo for $700 million.
- Channing Tatum launches Born and Bred American Vodka.

2018
- Luxardo Sour Cherry Gin, Gran Patrón Smoky Tequila, Bayou Rum, Nikka Japanese Whisky, Loch & Union American Dry Gin, Tequila Enemigo 00 Extra Añejo, and Haku Japanese Vodka are released.
- Elon Musk releases Tesla Tequila. The glass bottle is hand-blown and shaped like a lightning bolt. The bottle rests on a metal stand.
- Actor Ryan Reynolds purchases Aviation American Gin.

2019
- Nixta Licor De Elote Corn Liqueur, Copper & Kings "A Song For You" American Brandy, New York Distilling Company's Ragtime Rye Whisky and Dorothy Parker Rose Petal Flavored Gin, Camarena Añejo Tequila, Apologue Saffron Spiced Liqueur, Tod & Vixen's Dry Gin 1651, and Bearcat Infused Bourbon are released.
- Diageo acquires Seedlip, the world's first distilled non-alcoholic spirit.

2020
- BSB—Brown Sugar Bourbon, Air Vodka, Crystal Head Vodka Pride Edition, Teremana Tequila, Villa One Tequila, Barrell Bourbon Batch 003, and Midleton's Method and Madness Irish Whiskey are released.

- Bars around the world close and/or go out of business due to COVID-19. Batched to-go/pick-up cocktails become popular.
- Ina Garten (The Barefoot Contessa) goes viral after making a giant Cosmopolitan cocktail on Good Morning America.

2021 – Creamy Creation's Oats Liqueur, Havana Club Cuban Smoky Rum, The Louisville Bourbon Transit Co.'s Bedtime Bourbon, Tanqueray 0.0 Alcohol-Free Gin, Clean Co's Clean T Non-Alcoholic Oaky Agave Spirit, Eminente Cuban Rum, Broken Saddle Kentucky Straight Bourbon Whiskey, Baileys Deliciously Light Irish Cream, and 818 Tequila are released.

THE COCKTAIL WORLD TODAY— AND BEYOND

Between 2000 and 2010, the craft cocktail movement was in its infancy stage. Bar owners replicated the decor, style, fashion, and ambiance from either of two—significant—previous cocktail time periods: the first golden age of cocktails (1860–1919) or American Prohibition (1920–1933). Around 2010, bar owners had a light bulb moment and thought, "Hey! I don't have to look like an 1800s saloon or a speakeasy to produce fresh quality cocktails because that's the way cocktails should be made anyway." That self-realization (the message pioneers were trying to communicate all along) was the spark needed for millennials to create fresh cocktails for all other types of bars. In 2005, there were only around thirty fresh craft bars in all of America, and in 2018, there are over 500. The craft cocktail pioneers should be very proud of this achievement. What does the crystal ice ball predict for the future toddler, teenage, and adult stages of the second golden age of cocktails? Will robots replace bartenders? Will future bartenders become eco-conscious exploring ways to recycle the massive amounts of straws, cups, pics, and bottles dumped in landfills every day? Can bartenders cease stoking the embers of their wannabe-famous egos and simply live balanced lives, be good at their jobs, and understand the bottom line of hospitality? Will bars with fresh crafted cocktails be commonplace for the masses? Well, as for robots, probably not, because humans are social beings. Even high-tech futuristic fantasy shows such as *Star Trek*, which have the technological advances to build robot bartenders, choose not to. As millennials take over the cocktail wheel, it is safe to assume that they will follow their bartender ancestors' example—and boldly go where no one has gone before.

SHAKEN, NOT STIRRED: VODKA

A BRIEF HISTORY OF VODKA

Many drink historians place the origins of vodka anywhere from the 700s to the 1400s. However, most agree that it began somewhere in the "vodka belt." The vodka belt is located in Eastern, Central, and Northern Europe and includes countries such as Russia, Poland, and Ukraine.

Poland wins for finding the word "*wódka*" in court documents in the 1400s, but that word meant it was for medicines. Poland used the word "*gorzeć*" when vodka was for drinking. In 1534, a Polish pharmacist named Stefan Falimirz published *O Ziolach / O Mocy Ich* ("On Herbs and Their Potency"), which is believed to be one of the first documents containing the word "vodka." This luxurious illustrated book gave details for the preparation of over seventy vodka-based medicines.

Every country in the vodka belt had their own words for vodka and they translate into phrases such as "little water," "burnt water," "to burn," "ardent water," and "the water of life."

In 1789, Johann Tobias Lowitz developed charcoal filtration for vodka.

Before this, vodka tended to be infused with various fruits and herbs, so yes, it was flavored. Today, vodka is the number-one best-selling spirit in the world.

The Top Ten Things to Know About Vodka

1. Vodka can be made from any carbohydrate that is fermentable, not just potatoes.
2. Vodka can be made in any country of the world.
3. No one really knows who invented vodka. Most think it was Russia, but Poland seems to have more historical evidence.
4. The word "vodka" translates into "water."
5. Wolfschmidt was the first vodka introduced to America in the late 1800s.
6. The Moscow Mule was the first Smirnoff vodka cocktail marketed to America in the 1940s.
7. Vodka Martinis became extremely popular in America when the first James Bond film, *Dr. No*, was released in 1962.

8. While flavored commercial vodkas in the 1950s–1960s such as lime, grape, mint, and chocolate had some success, it wasn't until the 1980s when flavored vodkas rose to international success with the introduction of Absolut Peppar in 1984 and Absolut Citron in 1988.

9. If American vodka is made from sugarcane, then it must be distilled more than 95 percent abv (alcohol by volume) to be considered a neutral spirit and not rum.

10. Besides drinking, vodka can be used as a cleaning agent.

TYPES OF VODKA

There are two categories of vodka: flavored and plain. The plain category can be further categorized by what carbohydrate was used to make the vodka such as corn, wheat, potatoes, etc. The flavored category consists of plain vodka that has been flavored or infused with natural or artificial flavors.

Today, vodka companies like to brag about their water source, how many times their vodka has been distilled, or how many times it has been filtered.

POPULAR VODKA BRANDS

ABSOLUT
Produced in Ahus, Sweden, with Swedish water and winter wheat. Absolut introduced the first flavored vodka to America Absolut Peppar) in 1986. In 1988, they introduced Absolut Citron, which lead to the resurrection of the Cosmopolitan. Absolut has also been a prolific leader in the art and advertising world.

CRYSTAL HEAD
Produced in Newfoundland, Canada, with Canadian water and peaches-and-cream corn. It's distilled four times and filtered three times through diamond crystals. The bottle is shaped like a crystal skull head, but the drink is most known for being the brainchild of actor Dan Aykroyd.

GREY GOOSE
Produced in France with soft French winter wheat from Picardy, then shipped to Cognac to be mixed with spring water. Marketing master Sidney Frank created Grey Goose. Frank wanted to introduce the first luxury/super-premium vodka to America. It debuted in 1997.

HANGAR ONE

Produced in Alameda, California, with grains from the America Midwest and California-grown Viognier grapes. It is produced in an upcycled Navy aircraft hangar and distilled four times.

REYKA

Produced in Iceland with glacial Icelandic lava water, barley, and wheat in an eco-friendly distillery. They say that Iceland has the best water in the world.

DIFFERENT VODKA INGREDIENTS

The Ocean Organic vodka bottle is angled to emulate the Earth's axis like a globe. © *Hawaii Sea Spirits Organic Farm & Distillery*

- **Vodka made from corn**: Tito's, Crystal Head, Rain Organic, Pur, Deep Eddy, Prairie Organic and Iceberg.
- **Vodka made from sugarcane**: Firefly, Finlandia Raspberry, Ocean Organic, Cerén Organic, San Francisco Organic Beach, and Amazon Rainforest.
- **Vodka made from wheat**: Absolut, Grey Goose, Effen, Ketel One, Smirnoff, Reyka, Vox, Stoli, and Death's Door.
- **Vodka made from grapes**: Ciroc, Hangar One, Glass, Roth, and DiVine.
- **Vodka made from potatoes**: Chopin, Zodiac, Koenig Idaho, Prince Edward, Famous, and Chuckanut Bay.
- **Vodka made from honey**: Comb, 3 Bees, and Truuli Peak Alaskan.
- **Vodka made from apples**: Ironworks, Tree, and Untamed Irish.
- **Vodka made from barley**: Finlandia, Sipsmith, East Van, Maximus, and Valt Single Malt Scottish.
- **Vodka made from rye**: Belvedere, Shakers, King Peter, and Sobieski.

FUN VODKA FACTS

› The vodka 250,000 Scovilles Naga Chilli is the hottest vodka in the world. It has been infused with Naga Jolokia chillies, then packaged in a heavy glass bottle with industrial-grade sealing wire and a lead security seal, so you will need wire cutters to open it. Their website even suggests that you should not purchase it.

› In 1953, Ian Fleming created a fictional cocktail for James Bond in *Casino Royale* called a Vesper. It was the first cocktail to have both vodka and gin in its recipe.

› Vodka is lighter than water.

› Billionaire vodka is the most expensive vodka in the world. It costs $3.75 million for one bottle. It is filtered through diamonds, and the bottle is adorned with 3,000 diamonds.

› Broadway dancers have been known to soak their socks in vodka, then dry them overnight. The next day, the vodka-soaked socks fight foot fungi.

› In 2005, the *New York Times* did a blind taste test with twenty-one high-end vodkas and for fun threw in Smirnoff vodka. Smirnoff won.

3

MOTHERS RUIN: GIN

A BRIEF HISTORY OF GIN

Gin historians have discovered that juniper-based health tonics were first mentioned in the 1269 Dutch book *Der Naturen Bioememenitions* by Jacob van Maerlant te Damme.

In 1575, Lucas Bulsius changed his family name to Bols, moved to Amsterdam, and set up his own jenever distillery. It was a favorite drink among the British troops who were in the Netherlands for the Dutch War of Independence (1567–1609). They gave it a nickname: Dutch Courage. In 1600, Bols had earned a reputation and was a preferred supplier to the powerful Dutch East India Company. This gave him first dibs on spices and herbs to make his jenever. Jenever was mentioned in a 1623 English play called *The Duke of Milan*. Hundreds of small Dutch gin distilleries were in operation by the mid-1600s.

Pietr Blower, a Dutch émigré (self-exiled) made a special recipe of jenever in Barbados. He brought distillery equipment and cane seedlings from Brazil in 1637.

Mature juniper berries. © *Bildagentur Zoonar GmbH / Shutterstock*

In 1672, William of Orange (from Holland) became the King of England. William heavily influenced the widespread manufacture of gin in England by taxing imported spirits and then allowed anyone to produce gin without a license, which led to distillers using unclean water and toxic, inferior ingredients. Gin was the cheapest drink in town and began to be blamed for a rise in crime, social issues, accidents, and many deaths. London became a slum of crime filled with drunkards. All of this led to the "Gin Craze," "Gin Lane," the "Gin Act of 1736," and the "Gin Act of 1751." In 1721, one-quarter of London is used for the production and sale of gin. Nearly two million gallons are produced.

Between 1825 and 1829, the first lavish London gin palaces opened with opulent style. Charles Dickens wrote about them in 1836, calling them "perfectly dazzling when contrasted with the darkness and dirt we have just left."

In 1862, American bartender and author Jerry Thomas published the first known Gin Martini recipe, called Martinez, in the first known cocktail book. The gin listed for the Martini was Old Tom. In 1888, New Orleans bar owner Charles Ramos created the city's most popular gin cocktail, the Ramos Gin Fizz. It also called for Old Tom gin.

During American Prohibition (1920–1933) mobsters made a gin-like hooch by infusing bootlegged moonshine with dried juniper berries, and by the 1940s, gin was revamped into a glamorous spirit with the help of Hollywood movie stars and films.

The Top Ten Things to Know About Gin

1. Gin is English, but was inspired by Holland.
2. Holland made genever (also spelled jenever), and this is what the English tried to replicate.
3. Technically, one can say that gin was the first flavored vodka.
4. Gin was given to Dutch soldiers with the nickname "Dutch Courage."
5. William of Orange brought genever from Holland to England.
6. Many herbs and botanicals are used in gin, but the juniper berry imparts the predominant flavor.
7. England's first commercial gin was called Old Tom. It was a sweet gin much like genever.
8. In the 1700s, the English we're allowed to make gin without a license.
9. Gin can be made anywhere in the world.
10. Gin was the original base spirit used in the Martini. The Martini glass image is the most iconic cocktail culture symbol worldwide. Other popular gin cocktails include Tom Collins, Singapore Sling, Negroni, Ramos Gin Fizz, Gimlet, and Monkey Gland.

TYPES OF GIN

Gin can be made anywhere in the world, but the prominent countries that produce it include the United States, Japan, France, Spain, Sweden, Canada, Scotland, and Germany, as does the continent of Africa. There are four categories of gin: Genever, London Dry (or just Dry), Plymouth, and New Western.

GENEVER (JENEVER)

Genever was the first invented in Holland. It has a sweet, malty taste. Genevers break down into four more categories: Oude, jonge, korenwijn, and graajenever.

Oude and jonge can only be made and sold in Holland and Belgium.

Old Tom was first created in England, but falls into this category because it is considered a sweet gin.

LONDON DRY (DRY)

Most people think of this when gin is mentioned. Popular brands are Bombay, Beefeater, and Tanqueray. The taste is clean and dry and mixes well in cocktails.

PLYMOUTH

This category is for gins produced in Plymouth, England. Today, the city only produces one gin and its name is Plymouth. It tastes aromatic, earthy, and fruity.

NEW WESTERN

These new gins hit the market around the start of the New Millennium. Most of them would fall into the category of "dry," and the juniper seems to be on the back end instead of the front end. Examples include: Hendrick's, Aviation, and Martin Miller's.

FUN GIN FACTS

› Gin is just vodka after its first distilling. The herbs and botanicals are added during the second distilling. It is fair to say that gin is flavored vodka.

› Almost zero juniper is cultivated; it is mostly picked in the wild.

› Today, the Philippines consumes more gin than any country in the world (25 million annual cases).

› The most famous Martini quote is by American poet and writer Dorothy Parker: "I like to have a Martini, two at the very most; three, I'm under the table, four I'm under my host!"

› The most expensive gin is Watenshi at $2,500 a bottle. The bottles are filled with the evaporation (Angel's Share). It takes one hundred distillations to fill one bottle.

4

YO, HO, HO AND A BOTTLE OF... RUM

A BRIEF HISTORY OF RUM

Today, 80 percent of the world's rum is produced in the Caribbean. All spirits start with a plant, and rum starts with a species of grass called sugarcane. But it took sugarcane almost 10,000 years to make it to the Caribbean. And it wasn't until the mid-1800s when it started tasting decent. Up until then, it was harsh.

Here is the short story. We know sugarcane is indigenous to South Asia, and it is believed that the sweet grass was first domesticated on the island of New Guinea around 8000 BCE. India is known to have first extracted and crystallized the sugary plant around 350 CE, and from there trade merchants brought it to Africa and then Spain.

By the 1400s, there was a huge demand for the "sweet salt" (sugar) in Europe, so the Portuguese began planting sugarcane on the Island of Madeira. They soon realized that it was an extremely labor-intensive task in all processes of growing, harvesting, and production. Slaves were therefore imported. In 1493, Christopher Columbus attempted to bring sugarcane seedlings to the Caribbean, but they did not survive the voyage. Spanish conquistador Diego Velázquez was on the ship with Columbus and settled in Hispaniola (Dominican Republic, Haiti, and the tiny islands around them) to be of service to Spanish knight and soldier Nicolás Ovando y Cáceres, who a couple years later became the governor of the Indies.

1595 engraving with modern watercolor of African slaves processing sugarcane to make rum in Hispaniola. © *Everett Historical / Shutterstock*

In the 1501, Pedro de Atienza was the first to successfully import sugarcane seedlings to Hispaniola. He harvested his first crop four years later. In 1511, on behalf of Spain, Diego Velázquez conquered Cuba, bringing Hispaniola sugarcane with him. In 1518, a royal decree from Charles V (ruler of the Spanish and Holy Roman Empire) licensed 2,000 slaves to be imported to Hispaniola to work the sugarcane fields.

And in 1523, another royal decree imported 1,500 slaves to Hispaniola and 2,500 to other Caribbean islands such as Puerto Rico and Jamaica. The Portuguese took their production to Brazil and by the mid-1500s, there were almost 3,000 sugar mills. The Dutch started taking sugarcane seedlings to plant on any Caribbean island they could. Barbados and the islands around the Dominican Republic were among the first. By the 1600s, rum in daily rations was common for the Royal Navy.

In 1758, George Washington campaigned for the Virginia House of Burgess by offering free Barbados rum to voters, and he won. In the 1700s, the Caribbean Islands were losing money on their tobacco and cotton crops due to America growing their own, so switching to sugarcane crops solved this problem. Thus began a mass production of Caribbean rum.

In 1810, the first hospital in Sydney, Australia, was financed by local businessmen in return for a contract that licensed them to import 60,000 gallons of rum to sell. The hospital was called Rum Hospital. In addition, in 1862, Don Facundo Bacardi began filtering his Cuban rum through charcoal.

The Top Ten Things to Know About Rum

1. Early America was funded by rum sales. In 1657, the first rum distillery was built in Boston.
2. In 1664, a rum distillery was built in New York City.
3. The Royal British Navy gave sailors a daily ration of rum from 1731 until 1970.
4. Bacardi's first distillery was in Cuba, not Puerto Rico.
5. No one knows where the word "rum" came from.
6. Eighty percent of rum comes from the Caribbean, but it can be made anywhere in the world.
7. Rum is made from fermented sugarcane juice, sugarcane syrup, or sugarcane molasses, which comes from squeezing, cutting up, and mashing sugarcane stalks. To this day, in many parts of the world, the cane is still crudely harvested by hand with machetes.
8. "Rum and Coca-Cola" by the Andrews Sisters was the number-one song in 1945. The most popular rum cocktails are the Daiquiri, Mojito, Hurricane, Rum Punch, Mai Tai, Dark 'n Stormy, Cuba Libre, Zombie, Planter's Punch, Piña Colada, and Hot Buttered Rum.

9. Barbados Mt. Gay is the oldest rum company in the world. They have held the oldest surviving deed, dating back to 1703.

10. Brazil grows the most sugarcane in the world and has over 2,000 nicknames for rum.

TYPES OF RUM

There are six categories of rum: light (also called white, silver, or platinum), gold (also called amber), dark (also called black), añejo (also called aged or premium), overproof, and flavored.

LIGHT RUM

Some light rum is distilled and then poured directly into the bottle. This light rum (also called fresh rum) is raw. Fresh distilled rum contains trace amounts of hydrogen sulfide gas, which makes the rum taste harsh. This is probably close to the way rum tasted in the 1600s.

Most light rum is aged up to a year in oak barrels previously used for aging American and Canadian whiskey. Aging light rum gives it a better taste for a commercial market.

The most popular light rum in the world is Bacardi. Bacardi's distillery is located in San Juan, Puerto Rico, and produces 100,000 thousand gallons of rum a day. That amount equates to filling an Olympic-size swimming pool in one week!

GOLD RUM

Gold rum is light rum that has been aged in oak barrels until it reaches a golden color. The aging mellows the light rum, resulting in a light-to-medium-bodied rum. It is then filtered and poured into bottles.

DARK RUM

Dark rums are made from the thick black by-product of sugarcane called molasses. After distillation, they are aged in barrels.

AÑEJO RUM

Añejo is the Spanish word for "aged." Añejo rum is light rum that has been aged. There are no guidelines for how long to age rum, so the process ends when the rum master determines it is ready. The result is dark, smooth-sipping rum. Añejo rums are compared to Cognac.

OVERPROOF RUM

Overproof rum is just what it sounds like. To be considered overproof it has to be bottled 100 proof or more, which also means bottled at 50 percent alcohol by volume or more. The number-one overproof rum found in most bars is Bacardi 151.

FLAVORED RUM

Flavored rums are infused with a myriad of flavors. Almost every rum brand has a portfolio of flavored rums.

OTHER THINGS TO KNOW ABOUT RUM

RHUM VS. RUM

If you find yourself looking at rum labels, every once in a while you will see rum spelled "rhum." Rhum is short for rhum agricole, which just means that the rum in that bottle was made from fresh-squeezed sugarcane juice and not with by-products like molasses.

BRAZILIAN RUM

Brazilian rum is called cachaça (ka-SHAH-suh). It is only made from fresh-squeezed Brazilian sugarcane juice.

NAVY STRENGTH RUM

When you think of Navy strength rum, think overproof gunpowder test. See, the Royal British Navy used to give sailors a daily "tot" of rum. A tot is about eight ounces (one cup). To make sure the rum was not cut with water (its strength weakened) they would put some rum on gunpowder and attempt to ignite it, and if it ignited, the rum was over 114 proof (or over 57 percent alcohol).

FUN FACTS ABOUT RUM

› Rum has gone by many names such as: Barbados water, demon water, grog, kill-devil, Nelson's blood, rhumbooze, rumbowling, rumbullion, rumbustion, and splice the main brace.

› On January 15, 1919, at the U.S. Industrial Alcohol Company in Boston, Massachusetts, a cast-iron tank holding 400,000 gallons of molasses ruptured, creating a sixteen-foot-tall sticky tsunami through the Atlantic railway station, lifting a train off the track, injuring a hundred fifty people, killing twelve horses and twenty-one people, until it finally rested as a lake of molasses in North End Park.

› Bacardi has the largest rum distillery in the world, located in San Juan, Puerto Rico. If you visit by cruise ship, skip the expensive excursion to tour the distillery. Instead, just pay twenty-five cents to ride the ferry. You can see the distillery where the cruise ships dock.

› August is National Rum Month.

› Most rum is produced in the Caribbean and almost every island produces rum.

› Jamaica's Wray & Nephew overproof rum is the world's highest proof rum at 63 percent.

› In 1943, the Disney cartoon character Donald Duck drank cachaça, and in the same theater feature, *Saludos Amigos* (Spanish for "Greetings, Friends") Disney introduced a new character from Brazil named José Carioca.

› The most expensive rum is a 1940 bottle of J. Wray & Nephew. It is valued at $54,000.

5

SOUTH OF THE BORDER: TEQUILA

A BRIEF HISTORY OF TEQUILA

The history of tequila is a short one. In the 1300s, the Aztecs used the agave plant to make an alcoholic beverage called pulque. In 1531, Spanish settlers—with knowledge of distillation—distilled the pulque. They called it mexcalli (mezcal).

Farmers loading harvested blue agave for tequila production; 2013 Tequila; Jalisco, Mexico. © *T Photography / Shutterstock*

In 1758, Spain's King Ferdinand VI issued a land grant to Don Jose Antonio de Cuervo to cultivate the blue agave plant in the town of Tequila, Jalisco, Mexico. In 1795, Spain's King Carlos IV granted a permit to produce tequila commercially to his son Jose Guadalupe de Cuervo. (Spanish King Carlos III prohibited alcohol, so it took thirty-seven years to start commercial production). Tequila was known as "mezcal de Tequila" until 1893 and was sold by the barrel. Cuervo's first bottled tequila was sold in 1906. The Cuervo family in modern times is wicked wealthy.

Today there are over 2,000 brands of tequila. Celebrities who have their own tequila brands include George Clooney, Justin Timberlake, Sean Combs, Mario Lopez, Carlos Santana, and Sammy Hagar.

The Top Ten Things to Know About Tequila

1. Tequila is Mexico's national spirit and by law, it can only be produced in five Mexican states and nowhere else in the world.
2. The Margarita is Mexico's national cocktail.
3. Jose Cuervo was the first commercial tequila, and it is still the number-one seller of tequila in the world.
4. There are over 200 varieties of the agave plant, but the blue agave is king.
5. Mezcal (also spelled mescal) is made from many types of agave plants. The marketing ploy of adding an aphrodisiac worm into a bottle of mezcal

started in the 1940s and lasted through the 1990s. The worm was actually a moth larva that lives on agave plants in the caterpillar phase of life.

6. The agave plant heart (piña) is used to make tequila. A piña can weigh up to 200 pounds.

7. In the 1950s Herradura tequila—thanks to crooner superstar Bing Crosby—was the first 100 percent blue agave tequila to be introduced in America.

8. Americans tend to drink tequila as shots with salt and lime. Mexicans don't use salt and lime when shooting tequila.

9. Just as it takes a long time and much effort to produce rum from sugarcane, the process of making tequila is also labor-intensive, and is mostly done by hand.

10. The most popular tequila cocktails are the Margarita, Strawberry Margarita, Tequila Sunrise, Bloody Maria, Paloma, and the Prairie Fire shot.

TYPES OF TEQUILA

BLANCO

Blanco tequila is also referred to as silver, white, and platinum. Most times, blanco is distilled then poured straight into the bottle. However, blanco is allowed to be stored in stainless-steel tanks for up to sixty days before bottling.

REPOSADO

Reposado means "rested." It's blanco that has been aged between two and twelve months in wood barrels. The color after aging is a light gold.

AÑEJO

Añejo means "old." It is blanco has been aged between one and three years. The color after aging is a dark gold. Añejos will be very smooth, therefore making it a good sipping tequila.

EXTRA AÑEJO

This category was added in 2006. It's blanco that has been aged a minimum of three years.

JOVEN

Joven mean "young." It's blanco that has additives added to it such as coloring (to make it look aged), oak extract, and sugar. Jose Cuervo is a joven.

FUN TEQUILA FACTS

› National Tequila Day is June 24.

› The agave plant is not from the cactus family; it is from the lily family.

› The most expensive tequila is Ultra-Premium Ley .925 Pasion Azteca at $225,000 a bottle. It is expensive because the bottle is made from platinum and white gold. The company also produces another bottle with encrusted diamonds.

› One of the most popular quotes about tequila is: "One tequila, two tequila, three tequila, floor."

› The heart of the agave plant is called piña because it looks like a pineapple.

6

Whichever Way You Spell It: A Brief History of Whiskey/Whisky

Scotland and Ireland both have claimed to be the inventor of whiskey since the 1400s. Today, Ireland holds the record for the oldest licensed whiskey distillery in the world—Old Bushmills—established in 1608; however, Scotland first recorded whisky on June 1, 1495 in Scottish accounting records (in the Exchequer Rolls of Scotland), which said, "To Friar John Cor, by order of King James IV, to make aqua vitae VIII bolls of malt." Historians say that VIII equates to around 1,500 bottles, so this shows that making whiskey has been going on for a while. It is believed that the word "whisky" came from the Gaelic word "usquebaugh" (water of life) then shortened to "usque" (usky) and then "whisky."

Whiskey, like many spirits, was birthed out of convenience, portability, and preservation. It is much easier to travel with and store a bottle of whiskey than a keg of beer!

In the 1700s, America began making whiskey. During the Whiskey Rebellion of 1791–1794, grain farmers did not want to pay taxes to the U.S. government. The U.S. government won.

Today, whiskey is made all over the world. Individual countries have their own whiskey regulations, which oversee such things as ingredients having to be home-grown, proofs, and percentages.

The Top Ten Things to Know About Whiskey/Whisky

1. America and Ireland spell whiskey with an "e." Scotland and Canada spell whisky without an "e."
2. Scotland and Ireland still fight today over who first invented whiskey.
3. America produces five whiskeys: Bourbon, rye, blended, corn, and Tennessee.
4. Bourbon whiskey has been the official spirit of the United States since 1964.
5. One can say that whiskey is distilled beer.

6. Popular whisk(e)y cocktails include the Whiskey Sour, Irish Coffee, Old-Fashioned, Manhattan, Rob Roy, Rusty Nail, Mint Julep, Sazerac, Lynchburg Lemonade, and Blood and Sand.
7. Jack Daniel's is a Tennessee whiskey, not Bourbon.
8. Bourbon whiskey can only be produced in America, in any of the fifty states. It must be made with at least 51 percent corn, which must be American. No state except Kentucky can put "Kentucky Whiskey" on its label.
9. Whiskey is made from fermented grains such as corn, rye, wheat, and barley.
10. America's national Capitol Building was built with whiskey. In 1791, President George Washington imposed a whiskey tax to pay for its construction. Thomas Jefferson was opposed to the tax, calling it "big government tactics," then resigned as Secretary of State.

TYPES OF SCOTCH WHISKY

Scotland produces two types of whisky: single malt and blended. Scotch whisky can only be produced in Scotland, which has six whisky regions: Highlands, Lowlands, Speyside, Campbeltown, Islands, and Islay. Each region's whisky tastes different because of the soil. By law, all Scotch whisky must be aged a minimum of three years.

SINGLE MALT
Single malt means that the whisky comes from a single distillery. Many whisky barrels in a single distillery can be blended together, but that still means it is "single malt."

Another category that comes from a single distillery is called "single barrel." This means the whisky came from only one single barrel.

BLENDED
Blended Scotch whisky is a blend of single malts from several distilleries.

TYPES OF IRISH WHISKEY

Ireland only has four distilleries that produce single pot still and grain whiskey. By law, all Irish whiskey must be aged a minimum of three years. Currently, there are twelve whiskey distilleries in Ireland.

SINGLE POT STILL

Single pot still Irish whiskey breaks down into two categories: single pot still and single malt. Both must be made at a single distillery in a pot still. The only difference is that single malt must be made from 100 percent malted barley and single pot still is made with a combination of malted and unmalted barley.

GRAIN WHISKEY

Grain whiskey breaks down into two categories: blends and single grain. Grain whiskey is made in a column still, which means it can be made continuously. Single grain Irish whiskey is not common, but some brands make it available. Most of the single grain whiskey is used to make blends and some blends will be blended with single grain and pot stills.

TYPES OF AMERICAN WHISKEY

Every American should know that America produces five whiskeys: Bourbon, rye, blended, corn, and Tennessee. On May 4, 1964, congress declared Bourbon whiskey to be the official native spirit of the United States.

BOURBON

No one knows who produced the first Bourbon, or when it was produced. Bourbon whiskey can be made in any U.S. state and must be made with at least 51 percent American-grown corn. For the label to say "Kentucky Bourbon Whiskey" the whiskey must be made in Kentucky.

Bourbon Whiskey has two other categories: single barrel and small batch.

Single barrel Bourbon comes from one single barrel. Small batch Bourbon is made in small batches.

RYE

Rye whiskey must be made with at least 51 percent American-grown rye. In 1771, Sapling Grove, Tennessee, becomes the first business on record to make rye whiskey. The owner was a fifty-one-year-old Welsh-American named Evan Shelby.

BLENDED

Blended whiskey can be a blend of many grains; however, 20 percent must be straight (one grain). The two most popular brands are Seagram's 7 and Kessler's.

CORN

Corn whiskey is "moonshine." It is clear and unaged, and 80 percent of the grain must be corn. Today, they are making some high-end corn whiskey with more distillations and extra filtering. A couple of popular brands include Buffalo Trace White Dog and Hudson New York Corn.

TENNESSEE

Tennessee whiskey, as you might have guessed, must be made in Tennessee. From 1875 to 1997 there were only two Tennessee whiskey brands: George Dickel and Jack Daniel's. Jack Daniel's filters its whiskey through sugar maple tree charcoal (while other whiskeys are filtered through oak tree charcoal). Today, there are more brands to choose from that include Benjamin Prichard's Collier and McKeel, Nelson's Green Briar, and TenSouth. There are other brands that are produced in Tennessee, but they cannot be called Tennessee whiskey for multiple reasons, such as they are not aged, made from rye, or not charcoal-filtered.

TYPES OF CANADIAN WHISKY

For the most part, Canadians make blended whisky. They use several types of grains, and the whiskies produced have the reputation for being smooth. Most of Canada's distilleries are near the border of the United States, which came in handy during the American Prohibition.

Canadian Club Canadian whisky launched a "Hide a Case" ad campaign in 1967. Many cases of the whisky were hidden in places such as Mount Kilimanjaro, Mount St. Helens, and the Swiss Alps. Some have never been found.

OTHER COUNTRIES THAT MAKE WHISKEY/WHISKY

Countries that produce whiskey include Australia, India, Japan, New Zealand, South Africa, Spain, Sweden, Taiwan, and Wales.

Currently, Japan houses the world's largest whiskey distillery. It's called Fuji-Gotemba and is located in the foothills of Mount Fuji. The water used comes from melted snow.

FUN WHISKEY/WHISKY FACTS

› After serving as the first president of the United States, George Washington started a rye whiskey called Mt. Vernon. It is still in operation today.

› In 1874, while in Britain, Mark Twain drank a cocktail made of Scotch whisky, Angostura bitters, lemon juice, and crushed sugar before breakfast, before dinner, and before bed.

› One bottle of Glenlivet Winchester Vintage 1964 costs $25,000. The last Glenlivet descendant used American Bourbon oak barrels for aging.

› Third generation bartender, Sean Kenyon's favorite spirit is whiskey and he stocks plenty. He owns the award-winning speakeasy bookstore bar, Williams & Graham in Denver, Colorado (3160 Tejon Street). You enter through a secret bookcase.

› The steam engine was inspired by whisky distillation.

› Whiskey is the military word for the letter "W."

› Crown Royal Canadian Whisky was created for Queen Elizabeth's visit in 1939.

› The most sought-after American whiskeys are Pappy Van Winkle's twenty-three-year-old Bourbon (you can buy an empty bottle on eBay for $300) and George Washington's straight rye whiskey. Washington's whiskey can only be bought in person at the Shops at Mount Vernon in Mount Vernon, Virginia. Around three times a year a limited supply of small batch spirits are offered. The best thing to do is to get on their notification list at mountvernon.org.

Williams & Graham in Denver, Colorado. © *Greg Feldman / Phylum photography*

7

How Sweet It Is: Liqueurs

The history of liqueurs is brief. From what we know, liqueurs were first used for medicinal purposes. Monks were experimenting with liqueurs in the 1300s. One of the oldest liqueurs is Chartreuse.

Today, there are over 500 commercial liqueurs in the world made with various ingredients such as fruit, herbs, flora, spices, egg yolks, nuts, tea, coffee, honey, and even vegetables.

The Top Ten Things to Know About Liqueurs

1. Liqueurs are highly flavored sugar syrups with a spirit base.
2. Most liqueurs are low proof, but there are also high-proof liqueurs.
3. Cream liqueurs are made with dairy cream and have a shelf life of two years.
4. Crème (French pronunciation is Krem) liqueurs are syrupy and do not contain dairy cream.
5. Malibu rum is considered a liqueur because it is made with coconut flavor and sugar syrup.
6. In America, "schnapps," "cordial," and "crème" often mean the same thing as the word "liqueur." Liqueurs can be drunk on their own or used in cocktails to add a sweet flavor to the drink.
7. Contrary to popular belief, Southern Comfort is a liqueur, not a whiskey.
8. It took the creators of Baileys Irish Cream four years of experimentation to keep the cream from curdling with the whiskey. Baileys debuted in 1974.
9. Liqueurs are not always sweet. Some can fall into the "bitter" category.
10. The most popular cocktails made with liqueurs include Amaretto Sour, Black Russian, White Russian, Aviation, the Last Word, Nutty Irishman, Vieux Carré, Mudslide, Rusty Nail, Fuzzy Navel, Sex on the Beach, Melon Ball, Malibu & Pineapple, Appletini, Godfather, Godmother, Cosmopolitan, Jäger Bomb, Grasshopper, Pink Squirrel, and Harvey Wallbanger.

THE MOST POPULAR AND UNIQUE LIQUEURS FROM AROUND THE WORLD

Bols, Marie Brizard, and DeKuyper are the largest liqueur brands in the world. Each of these companies produces standard crème, cream, and schnapps flavors such as anisette, amaretto, banana, blackberry, blue Curaçao, butterscotch, cacao, cassis, cinnamon, melon menthe, pomegranate, raspberry, sour apple, sloe gin, strawberry, triple sec, and violette.

POPULAR LIQUEURS

- **Ancho Reyes:** Mexican ancho chili liqueur.
- **Baileys Irish Cream:** made with Irish whiskey, milk from Irish cows, chocolate, and vanilla.
- **Bénédictine:** French herbal liqueur.
- **Canton:** French ginger liqueur.
- **Chambord:** French black raspberry liqueur presented in beautiful sphere-shaped bottles.
- **Chartreuse:** high-proof French herbal liqueur.
- **Cherry Heering:** Dutch cherry liqueur.
- **Cointreau:** French orange liqueur.
- **Disaronno:** Italian almond amaretto liqueur.
- **Drambuie:** high-proof Scotch whiskey-based honey liqueur.
- **Fireball:** high-proof Canadian whisky cinnamon liqueur.
- **Frangelico:** Italian hazelnut liqueur that comes in a unique bottle shape that resembles a monk.
- **Galliano:** Italian anise-vanilla liqueur that comes in a very tall bottle.
- **Grand Marnier:** high-proof French Cognac–based orange liqueur.
- **Jack Daniel's Tennessee Honey:** American whiskey-based honey liqueur.
- **Jägermeister:** high-proof German herbal liqueur.
- **Kahlúa:** rum-based Mexican coffee liqueur.
- **Limoncello:** Italian lemon zest liqueur.
- **Luxardo Maraschino:** Italian Marasca cherry liqueur.
- **PAMA:** American pomegranate liqueur.
- **Pimm's Cup No. 1:** English gin-based herbal liqueur.
- **Southern Comfort:** high-proof American peach spice liqueur.

- **St. Germain:** French elderflower liqueur.
- **Sambuca:** high-proof Italian anise liqueur.
- **Tuaca:** high-proof brandy-based Italian vanilla-lemon liqueur.

UNIQUE LIQUEURS

- **Advocaat:** brandy-based Dutch liqueur made with eggs and sugar.
- **Akvavit:** high-proof Scandinavian liqueur made with caraway seeds.
- **Amarula:** South African cream liqueur made from the fruit of the marula tree. The fruit is picked in the wild, not cultivated. The marula is also called the elephant tree because elephants will bang against it to knock fruit off the tree.
- **AGWA:** high-proof liqueur made in Amsterdam. It contains herbs and Bolivian coca leaves. The coca leaves are picked in the Andes and then shipped under armed guard.
- **Cynar:** Italian bitter liqueur made with artichokes and herbs.
- **Goldschläger:** high-proof Swiss cinnamon schnapps that contains gold leaf flakes.
- **Killepitsch:** high-proof German liqueur that is made with ninety different fruits.
- **Tequila Rose:** tequila-based Mexican strawberry cream liqueur.
- **Umeshu:** sweet-and-sour Japanese liqueur made from unripe ume fruit. Ume is often nicknamed Chinese plums.
- **Visinata:** Russian liqueur made from sour cherries.

FUN LIQUEUR FACTS

› In 1977, Melon Balls (vodka, Midori melon liqueur, and orange juice) were served at the wrap party for the film *Saturday Night Fever* at Studio 54. This is when Midori was launched in America.

› The shape of a Frangelico hazelnut liqueur bottle is designed to resemble a friar in his habit—it comes with a rope tied around the bottle's waist.

› Goldschläger high-proof Swiss cinnamon schnapps contains fifty cents of real gold flakes in every bottle.

8

LIQUID BREAD: BEER

A BRIEF HISTORY OF BEER

No one knows exactly when or where beer was invented. Some believe that because beer and bread used the same ingredients, they must've happened around the same time.

Archaeologists and scientists have discovered ancient beer recipe tablets, beer residue inside pottery jars, poems mentioning beer, cave drawings depicting beer, beer drinking songs, and more.

From around 8000 BCE to 1000 CE, beer was warm, slightly thick, murky, and probably had particles floating in it. Hops became popular to use when making beer around 800 CE because it added flavor, bitterness, and, most importantly, helped with preservation. Up until the 1400s, beer was something one made at home. By the 1500s the brewing of beer had become commercialized. Beer ingredient laws were passed, lagers were accidently discovered, and beer was stored in cool places underground or in caves. The 1700s brought the Industrial Revolution and beer production soared.

Boilermaker drink: drop a shot of whiskey into a beer. © *Brent Hofacker / Shutterstock*

When the American Prohibition (1920–1933) started, it put 1,300 breweries out of the alcohol business, so they had to sell other products. Some sold ice cream and some used their equipment to make dyes. The large breweries such as Pabst, Schlitz, and Miller sold malt extract (what you needed to make beer at home), but they advertised it as a bread-making product.

In 1979, President Jimmy Carter made it legal to sell beer ingredients for home brewing, which kickstarted the microbrew movement of the 1980s. Today, America has over 4,000 breweries. Almost every big city offers several local beers in all types and styles.

The Top Ten Things to Know About Beer

1. Beer (or ale to be accurate) is the world's first known alcohol on record.

2. The Black Velvet beer-cocktail was invented in honor of Prince Albert in 1861. It was made with stout beer layered on top of champagne.

3. Beer breaks down into two categories: ale and lager. Ale uses top fermenting yeasts and lager uses bottom fermenting yeasts. Ales are ancient and lagers are only a couple hundred years old.

4. Beer uses the most types of glassware/vessels of any alcohol category. The largest is a yard and the smallest a half pint.

5. The most popular beer-cocktail shooters in the world include the Flaming Dr. Pepper, Boilermaker, and the Irish Car Bomb.

6. Beer also wins for using the most types of packaging/storage in various sizes. Examples include cans, glass and aluminum bottles, kegs, and casks.

7. The beer stein was invented in the 1300s and, 200 years later, lids were added to keep flies out of the beer.

8. The Anchor Steam brewery in San Francisco has been using both top and bottom fermenting yeasts in their beer since 1896.

9. The oldest operating brewery in America is Yuengling & Son.

10. A beer-cocktail called Hangman's Blood was mentioned in the 1929 novel *A High Wind in Jamaica*. Hangman's Blood consists of porter ale, rum, gin, whisky, port, and brandy. And in 1960, Anthony Burgess (*A Clockwork Orange*) wrote in the *Guardian* newspaper (England) about this same cocktail, "It tastes very smooth, induces a somehow metaphysical elation, and rarely leaves a hangover...I recommend this for a quick, though expensive, lift."

TYPES OF BEER

ALE

Individual households, small inns, and pubs (public houses) made ale from 8000 BCE to the 1400s. From the 1500s to the present, ale had been mostly made commercially. Styles of ales include stout, porter, bitter, brown, wheat, cream, lambic, and pale. Popular ale brands include Guinness, Newcastle Brown, Bass Ale, Redhook, Sam Adams Porter, Sierra Nevada Pale Ale, and Blue Moon.

LAGER

Produced in the Czech Republic in 1842, Pilsner Urquell was the first commercial pilsner lager. It is still made today. Most people think that all lagers have a clear yellow color, but this is untrue. Creating a lager has to do with the bottom fermenting yeast, time, and temperature. Styles of lager include pilsner, bock, dry, ice, dunkel, and amber. Popular lager brands include Budweiser (and all the others like Coors, Michelob, etc.), Stella Artois, Shiner Bock, Warsteiner Dunkel, Keystone Ice, Corona, and Negra Modelo.

CORONA COCKTAILS

In 1996, the Corona Limon became popular. It is easy to make—just pour a shot of Bacardi Limon rum in a Corona beer. Another popular Corona cocktail is a Corona Margarita where you insert an opened bottle of Corona into a large Margarita.

BEER WORDS TO KNOW

ABV - Alcohol by volume

FUN BEER FACTS

- Beer is just liquid bread.
- It has been said that Russia did not consider beer to be an alcoholic beverage until 2013.
- The world's most expensive bottle of beer, "Vieille Bon Secours," ale costs $1,000.
- A Scottish brewery makes the strongest beer in the world, called Snake Venom. Its alcohol content is 67 percent ABV. To compare, Budweiser has a 5 percent ABV.
- According to Wikipedia, the country that drinks the most beer in the world is the Republic of Nauru—formerly known as Pleasant Island—an island country in Micronesia in the Central Pacific.
- In 2012, Amsterdam starting paying alcoholics in beer to pick up trash in the streets.
- On October 17, 1814, in London, England, eight people drowned when the Meux and Company Brewery's beer vats burst, pouring almost 1.5 million liters of beer through the streets.

9

IT'S ALL ABOUT THE GRAPES: WINE

A BRIEF HISTORY OF WINE

In 2007, UCLA archaeologists found what appears to be a winery located in an Armenian cave that dates back to 4100 BCE. It contained grapevine remnants, drinking vessels, a wine press, and pottery jars for storage.

However, no one knows when wine was first invented. Many researchers think that it dates back to 6000 BCE. Art, archaeological digs, and writings show us that many civilizations used wine in ceremonies, religion, special occasions, medicinally, and in the home.

Engraving of Ancient Romans mixing wine and water in a large bowl. © *Oleg Golovnev / Shutterstock*

In the 1500s, wine was brought from Europe to South America. Wine production was attempted in Florida, Virginia, and Canada in the 1600s, but Spanish missions are responsible for bringing grapevines to California in the 1700s, which was the beginning of America's wine industry. By 1805, they established Sonoma's first winery. The Californian wine industry skyrocketed in the 1800s due to the Gold Rush and Europe's phylloxera problem. Phylloxera are microscopic bugs that eat grapevine roots. So for many decades, Europe could not produce wine.

Wine sales spiked again in the 1990s because craft microbrews were taking over the alcohol market and the wine industry wanted to compete. Up until then your wine choices at a restaurant were simply Burgundy, Chablis, or rosé, but in the 1990s restaurants were offering up to one hundred bottles of wine on their menus.

The Top Ten Things to Know About Wine

1. No one knows when wine was first invented.
2. Wine is made from fermented fruit. The most popular fruit used is grapes.
3. Even though there are over 10,000 varieties of grapes in the world, only around 300 are used for commercial wine.

4. Juice from all grapes is clear. It's the skins that give it color.
5. France and America are the top producers of wine, and all fifty U.S. states make wine.
6. "Appellation" means where (geographically) the grapes were grown.
7. "Vintage" means what year the grapes were harvested.
8. It takes about 600 grapes to make a bottle of wine, and there are 50 million bubbles in a bottle of champagne.
9. On Thanksgiving, Americans drink more wine than on any other day of the year.
10. The most popular cocktails made with wine include French 75, Sangria, Champagne Cocktail, Wine Spritzer, Kir, Kir Royale, Mulled Wine, Americano, Martini, and Manhattan.

TYPES OF WINE

Basically, all wine falls into two categories: red and white. From there they break down into still, sparkling, and fortified.

RED WINE

Red wine is made from black grapes. Black grapes have a reddish-bluish color. The grape skins are used during production. To make pink-colored wines like rosé and white Zinfandel, the skins are left on for a little bit then discarded. Popular commercial red grapes are Cabernet, Merlot, Pinot Noir, Zinfandel, and Beaujolais.

WHITE WINE

White wine is made from grapes that appear light green. White wine can also be made from black grapes if the skins aren't used. Popular commercial white grapes are Chardonnay, Pinot Grigio, Riesling, and Sauvignon Blanc.

FORTIFIED WINE

"Fortified" means ingredients such as sugar, brandy, herbs, or botanicals have been added to the wine. These include sherry, port, Madeira, and vermouths. The first three are often referred to as dessert wines.

ALL ABOUT BUBBLY (CHAMPAGNE, PROSECCO, CAVA, AND OTHER SPARKLING WINES)

Sparkling wine is the number-one alcoholic beverage used to celebrate occasions such as weddings, birthdays, and anniversaries. Just like Post-it notes, Super Glue, and penicillin, sparkling wine is a result of a happy accident.

Northern France (Champagne region) has a short growing season, and during the winter, fermentation would stop inside the wine bottles. As spring approached, the temperature rose, fermentation started again, and the bottles of wine would burst. A French Bénédictine monk named Dom Pérignon spent most of his adult life—until he died in 1715—trying to figure out a way to stop the bubbles.

By the early 1800s, the House of Veuve Clicquot (which was run by a woman) worked out a lot of champagne's issues by using thicker bottles, better corks, and riddling (getting out the sentiment in the bottom of the bottle). Countries such as Italy, Spain, and the United States. thereafter began putting the word "champagne" on their sparkling wine labels, which sparked the Champagne Wars. In 1919, laws were passed mandating that only champagne produced in the Champagne region of France could use the word "champagne" on its label. Today, Italy labels its sparkling wine as "prosecco"; Spain labels it as cava; and the United States just uses the term "sparkling wine."

WINE WORDS TO KNOW

- **Blend**: a blend of different wines.
- **Body**: weight and fullness of a wine, which you can discern when you have it in your mouth.
- **Bordeaux**: the area in Southwest France that is considered one of the best wine-producing regions in the world.
- **Brut**: French for "dry."
- **Demi-sec**: French term meaning "half dry."
- **Finish**: the taste in your mouth after swallowing wine.
- **Sulfites**: a natural by-product of the wine fermentation process.
- **Tannin**: Grape skins contain tannins, and the taste is dry or astringent like a strong cup of tea.
- **Varietal**: the main grape the wine is made from.
- **Vintage**: the year the grapes were harvested.

FUN WINE FACTS

› Champagne comes in eight bottle sizes. The largest is called Nebuchadnezzar and is equal to twenty standard 750 ml bottles.

› In 1863, French chemist Angelo Mariani infused Bordeaux **wine** with three types of coca leaves in the bottle and called it Vin Tonique Mariani. Two ounces contained twelve milligrams of cocaine. It was technically sold as a medicine that worked as an appetite suppressant, stomach stimulant, and helped with depression. It won a Vatican Gold Medal after Pope Saint Pius X and Pope Leo XIII endorsed it. In addition, it is believed that there were over 7,000 endorsements written by physicians. In 1884, John Pemberton from Atlanta, Georgia, replaced the **wine** with cola extract and soda and Coca-Cola was born.

› During the American Prohibition, grape juice concentrate was sold with instructions for how not to let it ferment—basically, telling consumers how to make **wine** at home.

› James Bond may be known for Vodka Martinis, but in the novels and films, he drinks champagne more than any alcohol.

› If a **wine** bottle is corked with real cork, then store the bottle on its side so the cork does not dry out.

› Be careful when opening a bottle of champagne and never point the cork at a person or a breakable object, because the cork can come out at 100 mph.

› Madeira is mentioned in William Shakespeare's play *Henry IV, Part One*, when Falstaff is accused of trading his soul for a chicken leg and a chalice of Madeira.

› In 2004, the hit independent film *Sideways* had bartenders' tongues turning sideways saying Pinot Noir one hundred times a night.

› Every third week in November, you can consume a sense of unity with the world by drinking the same **wine**—at the same time—with your global brothers and sisters. It is called "It's Beaujolais Nouveau Time!" Beaujolais Nouveau (BOH-zoh-LAY NO-voo) is bottled six to eight weeks after harvest and is distributed around the world within a week. This allows the opportunity to share the experience. Look up at the moon while drinking and you will share two experiences at the same time.

› The world's largest **wine** bottle is the sign for the Boondocks Lounge in Tucson, Arizona.

10

What to Drink Before and After Dinner: Aperitifs and Digestifs

A BRIEF HISTORY OF APERITIFS

An aperitif (uh-PAIR-uh-TEEF) is a before-dinner drink meant to stimulate the appetite. It's also a perfect way to socialize before dinner. No one knows the exact moment in history this ritual started, but it was all the rage in the late 1700s through the early 1900s.

The two countries that have embraced aperitifs the most are France and Italy. France spells it "aperitif" and Italy spells it "aperitivo." Today, those who like to partake of this before-dinner ritual agree and disagree on what makes a proper aperitif. The general rule is that it should be light, crisp, and refreshing.

POPULAR APERITIFS FROM AROUND THE WORLD

Popular spirits drunk in aperitif cocktails, and also on their own, include Aperol, Campari, Cynar, and Pimm's No. 1. Popular aperitif cocktails include the Pimm's Cup, Campari and soda, and Aperol and soda.

FORTIFIED WINE-BASED APERITIFS

Lovely wine-based bubbly aperitifs include champagne, prosecco, and cava.

Other light wine-based aperitifs include fino sherry, tawny port, Lillet, Lillet Rose, and light (dry) vermouths such as Cocchi Americano, Cocchi Americano Rosa, Dolin Blanc, and Noilly Prat dry.

Popular wine-based aperitif cocktails include the Champagne Cocktail, Wine Spritzer, and an Americano made with dry vermouth.

A BRIEF HISTORY OF DIGESTIFS

Italian limoncello liqueur. © *Gudrun Muenz / Shutterstock*

Digestifs are after-dinner drinks meant to help with digestion. Digestifs tend to be heavier and sometimes sweeter than aperitifs. No one knows when this drinking custom started, but it's fair to assume that experimenting with beverages to help settle one's stomach after a large meal has been a continuous venture.

Drinking digestifs in restaurants is not popular in America, mostly because restaurants look to turn tables for maximum sales. Europeans, on the other hand, embrace digestifs. They tend to relax and linger after a large meal.

POPULAR DIGESTIFS FROM AROUND THE WORLD

Each country tends to have its favorite digestif. In Italy it's limoncello; Germany, schnapps; Greece, ouzo; and Mexico, añejo tequila.

Other popular digestifs include absinthe, Chartreuse, Calvados, Sambuca, aged whiskeys, añejo rum, Fernet, Grand Marnier, and B&B. Popular digestifs cocktails include the Brandy Alexander, Grasshopper, Absinthe Drip, Rusty Nail, and Sazerac.

FORTIFIED WINE-BASED DIGESTIFS

Heavy wine-based digestifs include cream sherry, ruby port, Cognac, armagnac, grappa, pisco, and sweet vermouths such as Antica Formula Carpano, Cocchi Vermouth di Torino, Dolin Rouge, and Cinzano Rosso.

Popular wine-based digestif cocktails include the Manhattan, Rob Roy, Blood and Sand, Vieux Carré, and Negroni.

FUN APERITIF AND DIGESTIF FACTS

> Up until 2006, Campari got its red color from carmine dye that comes from an insect called the Armenian cochineal. Their bodies are dried then turned into a powder and then boiled in ammonia. This ancient coloring is still used today in lipsticks, eye shadows, ice cream, yogurt, and many products that are pink/red in color. In America it is required to list the ingredient on the label as carmine or cochineal extract.

> The Lillet (luh-LAY) used in James Bond's Vesper is no longer available, but the best substitute is Cocchi (ko-KEY) Americano.

> Grappa and pisco are pomace spirits. Pomace (also called "must") are the remains from wine making that includes, stems, seeds, skins, pulp, and anything else left from pressing grapes for wine. Grappa is made in Italy and pisco in Peru and Chile.

> Rémy Martin's King Louis VIII Cognac costs around $2,200 a bottle, and the bottle is made of crystal. Very high-end bars will carry it. It was seen and mentioned in the 1988 film *Cocktail*, Rihanna mentioned it in a 2015 song, it was mentioned on the TV show *The Larry Sanders Show*, and it shows up in many rap songs by artists such as Young Jeezy, Young Buck, Lil Wayne, T-Pain, and Yung Joc.

The Green Fairy:
All About Absinthe

A BRIEF HISTORY OF ABSINTHE FROM THE 1790S TO THE 1860S

Artemisia absinthium (a.k.a. grand wormwood) is an herb that grows wild in Switzerland and France, and has been used medicinally for thousands of years because of its acclaimed virtues as a digestive aid and nerve tonic.

Henri-Louis Pernod and Henri Dubied opened the first commercial absinthe distillery in Couvet, Switzerland, near the French border in 1797. They relocated to Pontarlier, France, in 1805, whereupon the Pernod Fils distillery became the world's largest producer of absinthe, and would retain that position until it was disbanded following the French absinthe ban in 1915.

During the French conquest of Algeria (1830–1847), soldiers were issued rations of absinthe because it was believed to prevent malaria and other diseases associated with unclean water. French soldiers returning from their service carried their taste for absinthe home with them, and absinthe soon became the fashionable drink of cafés that catered to the bourgeoisie.

A BRIEF HISTORY OF ABSINTHE FROM THE 1860S TO THE PRESENT

Beginning in the 1860s, the insect responsible for phylloxera began ravaging the vineyards of continental Europe. The plague particularly affected France, and was commonly referred to as the Great French Wine Blight. France even offered a cash prize to anyone who could cure the blight. Three botanists were called in to find a solution. In the meantime, however, the grape harvest declined and the price of wine rose accordingly. It was during this time that the popularity of absinthe increased, becoming the preferred tipple of the common people. The increased demand saw yearly increases in production, the price was lowered, and absinthe emerged as a nationally fashionable drink and object of global commerce.

Ted A. Breaux at the Combier Distillery in Saumur, France, cleaning an antique absinthe still, following a distillation of Jade absinthe; 2014. © *Ted A. Breaux*

Nearly thirty years would pass before the wine industry recovered from the widespread blight, but the masses were now hooked on absinthe. Famous artists, poets, and writers praised the virtues of the green spirit, and even nicknamed it La Fée Verte (the Green Fairy). Its popularity had crossed oceans by this point—a bar on Bourbon Street in New Orleans was opened in 1874 that would become the Old Absinthe House. One can still visit this bar and view the original built-in absinthe fountains on the backbar.

So why (starting in the 1900s) was absinthe beginning to be banned worldwide? Because the wine industry promoted the notion that absinthe was a poison, aiming to specifically demonize grand wormwood, in attempts to recover its lost market share. Both the wine industry and the temperance movement capitalized upon the cheap, adulterated versions of the drink imbibed by poor alcoholics in an effort to smear the entire category. This attack was promoted by a well-funded publicity campaign that advertised absinthe as a source of moral corruption and the ruin of modern society.

In America, absinthe was banned from 1912 to 2007, which created an unfilled void when it came to classic cocktails that called for the spirit. After unraveling almost a century's worth of falsehoods and myths, New Orleans native and chemist Ted A. Breaux and Viridian Spirits, LLC, obtained approval to introduce Lucid Absinthe Supérieure as the first genuine absinthe sold in the American market in ninety-five years.

The Top Ten Things to Know About Absinthe

1. "Absinthe" is a French word that means "wormwood." Wormwood is an herb that can have convulsive properties if used to excess.
2. Absinthe is pronounced AB-sent.
3. Pernod (purr-NO) was the very first commercial absinthe.
4. Absinthe does not make you hallucinate.
5. Green Fairy is a nickname for absinthe.
6. La fée verte is French for Green Fairy.
7. Absinthe was banned in America in 1912.

8. New Orleans native, chemist, and absinthe historian Ted A. Breaux and Viridian Spirits, LLC, are responsible for bringing absinthe back to America in March 2007. They spent $500,000 to get the Alcohol and Tobacco Tax and Trade Bureau (TTB) to drop the American ban on absinthe.
9. Historic partaking of absinthe does not include setting anything on fire.
10. The real reason absinthe was banned is because the wine industry wanted their business back.

FIVE POPULAR ABSINTHE COCKTAILS

When using absinthe in a cocktail, two challenges are posed. One is that its prominent flavor is anise, which some casually associate with "black licorice." The other is that it's very high-proof.

ABSINTHE BLOODY MARY

This absinthe drink may sound odd, but the herbs in the absinthe actually go well with the herbs and spices in the Bloody Mary mix.

The Recipe

Pour the following ingredients into a tall 12-ounce glass:

- 1.5 ounces absinthe
- 5 ounces Bloody Mary mix

Add ice, stir, then garnish as you choose.

ABSINTHE SUISSESSE

Believed to be invented at the Old Absinthe House in New Orleans.

The Recipe

Chill a cocktail glass, then pour the following ingredients into a blender:

- 1.5 ounces absinthe
- 1 egg white
- .5 ounce orgeat syrup
- Half-cup ice
- .5 ounce heavy cream

Blend for five to ten seconds, then pour into a chilled cocktail glass.

THE ABSINTHE DRIP

In the first hundred years of absinthe's existence, it was drunk as an Absinthe Drip. An Absinthe Drip requires six things: absinthe, a glass, a slotted absinthe spoon, a sugar cube, an absinthe fountain, and ice-cold water.

The Recipe

- 1 ounce absinthe
- 5 ounces ice water

- 1 sugar cube

First, take the glass of your choice and add six ounces of water so you can eyeball how high you'll need to drip the water. Pour out the water and dry the glass. Next, fill an absinthe fountain with ice and water. Now pour the absinthe into the glass, set a slotted absinthe spoon across the rim, then place the sugar cube on top. Position this setup under the spigot of the absinthe fountain and then slowly drip water over the sugar cube until it melts and you have reached the six-ounce level. Stir and enjoy.

As the water mixes with the oil in the absinthe, it will turn cloudy. There are all kinds of absinthe glasses, spoons, fountains, and more that you can purchase. It all depends on how far you want to take your Absinthe Drip experience.

OBITUARY COCKTAIL

This cocktail was invented at the oldest bar in New Orleans, Lafitte's Blacksmith Shop.

The Recipe

Chill a cocktail glass, and then in a mixing glass add the following:

- .25 ounce absinthe
- 2 ounces gin

- .25 ounce dry vermouth

Add ice, then stir and strain into a chilled cocktail glass.

DEATH IN THE AFTERNOON

It is said that in Spain, Ernest Hemingway invented this cocktail while writing his nonfiction bullfighting book of the same name. One thing is for sure—it is lethal.

The Recipe

In a chilled champagne glass add:

• **1 ounce absinthe**

• **5 ounces chilled champagne**

Absinthe drip fountain at the Bourbon O Bar on Bourbon Street. © *Brian Huff*

12

An Essential Ingredient: Bitters

A BRIEF HISTORY OF BITTERS

No one knows the exact time when bitters started, but it's agreed that it was first used medicinally. In 1712, Richard Stoughton, a British clergyman, received a patent for Magnum Elixir Stomachicum, which was an alcohol-based herbal infusion. It was the second compound medicine in the world to receive a patent. Soon, the public was calling it Stoughton's Bitters. In 1730, he exported it to America.

Bitters is made of selected herbs, spices, seeds, dried fruit peels, flora, barks, botanicals, or roots of one's choice—a witch's brew of sorts—then preserved in a base of high-proof alcohol. However, some bitters are nonalcoholic and made with glycerin. In the 1800s, these elixirs were advertised as cure-alls and sold in 750 ml bottles. Today, due to the cocktail revolution, there is a huge assortment of bitters on the market just like there was back in the 1880s. Bitters can be dashed into fizzy water and drunk to calm a stomachache, and you can use bitters in food and drinks to add flavor. Bitters doesn't taste bitter as the name implies. When used in cocktails, it simply adds a dash of concentrated flavor. Most say it seasons the cocktail in the same way salt seasons food. The best way to taste test bitters is through your nose. No, do not sniff. Dash a couple drops in your palm, rub your palms together, then cover your nose and mouth and smell.

If you'd like to experiment with making your own medicinal bitters, then these herbs and other plants may be worth exploring: amla berry, ashwagandha, astragalus root, bamboo stem, burdock root, Bupleurum, dandelion root, ellagitannin, fo-ti, gotu kola, gubinge, holy basil, Indian gooseberry, Japanese knotweed, jiaogulan, kudzu leaf, licorice root, maca, mallow leaf, moringa leaf, pine bark, pine needles, pine pollen, red clover, rosehip, sea buckthorn, Siberian ginseng, suma, watercress, and yellowdock root.

ANGOSTURA BITTERS

Since 1824, Angostura bitters has stood the test of time. In 1862, Don Carlos Siegert from Trinidad first exhibited it at the Great London Exposition. The cocktail Pink Gin was invented at the same time, and was called Amargo Aromatico. Angostura bitters won a medal at the 1873 World's Fair in Vienna, Austria. Many cocktails call for the bitters, including the Champagne Cocktail, Vieux Carré, Pisco Sour,

Old-Fashioned, Pink Gin, Manhattan, Rob Roy, Singapore Sling, Planter's Punch, and Zombie.

PEYCHAUD'S BITTERS AND BOKER'S BITTERS

Johann Boker created Boker's bitters in 1828 and one hundred years later, it went extinct. Adam Elmegirab re-created Dr. Adam Elmegirab's Boker's Bitters in 2009. © *Adam Elmegirab*

The next two most popular bitters in the 1800s were Peychaud's Bitters (1857) from New Orleans and Boker's (1828) from New York. Peychaud's is the red bitters used in a Sazerac or Vieux Carré cocktail. If you ever visit New Orleans, just pop into the local grocery store and take a bottle or two home with you. Boker's bitters was found in many cocktail recipe books before becoming extinct, but thankfully it has been raised from the dead by Dr. Adam Elmegirab's Bitters. Some of the vintage cocktails that called for Boker's include the Japanese Cocktail, Martinez, Manhattan, and Crusta.

ORANGE BITTERS AND FEE'S BITTERS

Orange bitters was called for in the first known Martini recipe seen in print, in 1862. After Prohibition until the early 2000s the only bitters available was Angostura. When Regans' Orange Bitters No. 6 was produced in 2005 by cocktail author, historian, and bartender Gary Regan, it opened the bitters floodgate. Fee's Bitters, who had been in business in Rochester, New York, from 1835, also saw a decline in sales when Prohibition began, so they focused on altar wines and continued with wine until the 2000s when the cocktail culture started to flourish. As of 2016, Fee's now offers seventeen types of bitters, botanical waters, syrups, and more.

BITTERS BOTTLES

You may have noticed many little bottles all around the drink-making station of your local bar. Those are bitters bottles. Some will be purchased bitters and some will be made from scratch by your bartenders.

Modern bitters bottles on bartop. © *GKondor83 / Shutterstock*

Today, there are too many bitters companies to mention and many bartenders are making their own bitters. Never in the history of the cocktail culture has there been so many flavors to choose from. Check out these flavors: Gumbo, Tex-Mex, Memphis BBQ, Holiday Pie, Figgy Pudding, Mi Casa, Creole, Celery Shrub, Hellfire, Winter Melon, Orange Cream, Hoped Grapefruit, Jamaican Jerk, Cherry Bark, Blackstrap, Roasted Macadamia, Wild Mountain Sage, Palo Santo, Vanilla Chai, Hair of the Dog, Bitter Frost, Smoked Chili, and Wormwood Bitters.

Some of the top companies producing bitters around the world include AZ Bitters Lab, Basement Bitters, Bittercube Bitters, Bitter End Bitters, Bittered Sling Bitters, Dr. Adam Elmegirab's Bitters, Dram Bitters, El Guapo Bitters, Fees's Brothers Bitters, Hella Bitter, Old Men Bitters, Scrappy's Bitters, the Bittered Truth Bitters, the Cocktail Experiment Bitters, and Urban Moonshine Organic Bitters.

DIGESTIVE BITTERS

There are also spirits that have bitter qualities, and many countries have their own. They are measured into cocktails in ounces, not dashes. The most popular include Amer Picon, Aperol, Averna, Becherovka, Campari, Cynar, Fernet, Branca, and Jägermeister.

HOMEMADE BITTERS PREPARATION

Before you turn your kitchen into a DIY bitters lab, it is best to prepare.

Here are some items to gather:

- A few quart-sized Mason jars.
- Any high-proof liquor (80 proof or higher). A lot of beginners like to start with vodka because it's neutral. But later you can try other spirits such as whiskey and tequila. Just keep in mind they will add to the flavor.
- Filters of some sort like cheesecloth, a fine strainer, or a coffee filter.
- Small dropper or bitters bottles of your choosing.
- Fancy or plain labels of your choosing, or just use masking tape.

- A small funnel to fit into the small bottles.
- Your choice of herbs, spices, seeds, dried fruit peels, whole fresh fruit, flora, botanicals, roots, etc. To help you get started think dried fruit, dried citrus peels, dried flora, coffee beans, peppercorn, star anise, cracked whole nutmeg, juniper berries, cherry bark, etc. Barks may be easier to find online.
- Once you hunt and gather your ingredients, put them in the jar and fill with the spirit. It will need to infuse for several weeks to draw out the flavor. Each day you should agitate the jar to mix up everything. When ready, strain the mixture into another jar using cheesecloth or a very fine strainer. Some people with use both.
- The solids that you catch in the strainer then need to be put into a pot with some water and brought to a boil, then simmered for fifteen minutes. Put all of that mixture into a separate jar and let sit for one week.
- When ready, strain out the solids. The solids can be thrown away. Combine the two jars of liquid you've created, and if the end result has sediment in the bottom or floating in the mixture, you'll need to strain it again.
- Lastly, you can add a little sweetener to make it more palatable. You can use honey, maple syrup, molasses, or rich simple syrup (two parts sugar to one part water dissolved into a syrup). Shake it all up, and now you are ready to bottle.

HOMEMADE BITTERS RECIPES

Here are some basic recipes to get you started:

BASIC BITTERS

Makes 16 ounces

- Pinch cardamom
- Pinch caraway
- Pinch coriander seeds
- 1 cup dried bitter orange peel
- 2 cups grain alcohol
- 2 tablespoons honey

Combine all the ingredients into a sterilized jar with a lid and allow to sit in a cool dark place for three weeks, agitating it every day. When ready, strain through cheesecloth or a fine strainer into another jar. Bring the solids caught in the strainer to a boil with water and then simmer for fifteen minutes. Put all that mixture into a lidded jar and allow to sit for one week. When ready, strain and combine with the first strained jar. Add the sweetener, shake, and then funnel into dropper or bitters bottles.

BOURBON PECAN BITTERS

Makes 16 ounces

- 1/2 cup roasted pecans
- 2 whole cloves
- 1 cinnamon stick
- 1 vanilla bean, split
- 1 tablespoon wild cherry bark
- 1 tablespoon gentia root
- 2 cups high-proof Bourbon
- 2 tablespoons maple syrup

Combine all the ingredients into a sterilized jar with a lid and allow to sit in a cool dark place for three weeks, agitating it every day. When ready, strain through cheesecloth or a fine strainer into another jar. Bring the solids caught in the strainer to a boil with water and then simmer for fifteen minutes. Put all that mixture into a lidded jar and allow to sit for one week. When ready, strain and combine with the first strained jar. Add the sweetener, shake, and then funnel into dropper or bitters bottles.

LAVENDER BITTERS

Makes 16 ounces

- 1 cup dried lavender
- 1/2 cup orange peels
- 1 vanilla pod, split

- 2 cups grain alcohol
- 2 tablespoons agave nectar

Combine all the ingredients into a sterilized jar with a lid and allow to sit in a cool, dark place for three weeks, agitating it every day. When ready, strain through cheesecloth or a fine strainer into another jar. Bring the solids caught in the strainer to a boil with water and then simmer for fifteen minutes. Put all that mixture into a lidded jar and allow to sit for one week. When ready, strain and combine with the first strained jar. Add the sweetener, shake, and then funnel into dropper or bitters bottles.

ORANGE BITTERS

Makes 16 ounces

- 1 cup orange peels
- 2 cardamom pods
- Pinch coriander seeds
- 1 teaspoon fennel seed

- 10 drops gentian extract
- 2 cups grain alcohol
- 2 tablespoons rich simple syrup

Combine all the ingredients into a sterilized jar with a lid and allow to sit in a cool, dark place for three weeks, agitating it every day. When ready, strain through cheesecloth or a fine strainer into another jar. Bring the solids caught in the strainer to a boil with water and then simmer for fifteen minutes. Put all that mixture into a lidded jar and allow to sit for one week. When ready, strain and combine with the first strained jar. Add the sweetener, shake, and then funnel into dropper or bitters bottles.

13

What Exactly Is a Cocktail Mixer? A Guide to Making Your Own

Mixers are generally nonalcoholic ingredients that provide balance and flavor when mixed with alcohol to create a cocktail. Just remember: to make the best-tasting cocktail, always go fresh.

LIST OF COCKTAIL MIXERS

JUICES

The main juices most bars stock include cranberry, grapefruit, lemon, lime, orange, and pineapple. Other juices that bars could offer include apple, carrot, clam, olive, pomegranate, and tomato.

CARBONATED SODA

The main sodas most bars stock include cola, diet cola, ginger ale, lemon-lime, soda water, tonic water, and Perrier. Other sodas that bars could offer include Dr. Pepper, root beer, ginger beer, and anything they would need for a special cocktail on the menu.

SWEETENERS

Unless you are rimming a glass edge or making an Old-Fashioned the old-fashioned way, sugar behind the bar is mostly used in a liquid state called "simple syrup." This is because the liquid mixes better in cocktails than granulated sugar. Many bars make their own simple syrup because it's easy! To make two cups of simple syrup, all you need is one cup of granulated sugar and one cup of warm to hot water. Mix in a blender or a saucepan until the sugar dissolves and you've made simple syrup. This syrup can be kept in the refrigerator for a month.

Other sweeteners a bar can stock include agave nectar, coconut cream, grenadine, gomme syrup, honey, orgeat syrup, pureés, or any flavored syrup the bar needs for certain cocktails on their menu.

DAIRY

The most common dairy mixer behind bars is half-and-half (half milk and half cream). Other dairy mixers that could be found behind bars are cream, eggs, eggnog, ice cream, and unsalted butter. Some bars carry nondairy plant-based options that include soy milk, almond milk, rice milk, and coconut milk.

OTHER MIXERS

Other popular mixers behind a bar include Bloody Mary mix, strawberry mix, Margarita mix, Piña Colada mix, sweet-and-sour mix, apple cider, coffee, tea, hot chocolate, hot water, and apple cider vinegar. The first five mixers mentioned can be purchased, but those products are low-quality fake options. It's best to make them yourself.

ADDED INGREDIENTS

Many added ingredients can be added, stirred, or shaken into a cocktail to enhance the flavor and texture. Some of these include, spices, herbs, and sauces such as steak sauce, Worcestershire, and hot sauce.

HOMEMADE COCKTAIL MIXER RECIPES

SIMPLE SYRUP

Have you ever tried to mix a spoonful of sugar in your iced tea only to find the sugar at the bottom of the glass? This is why it's easier to mix syrups into cocktails. Simple syrup is the base of all syrups and it's very easy to make. If you want to avoid sugar and need a low glycemic option then try Markus Sweet, Monkfruit sweetener, stevia, or xylitol sweet.

Makes 2 cups

- 1 cup water, hot or boiling
- 1 cup granulated sugar of your choice

Now, there are a few ways you can combine the water and the sugar to create simple syrup. Just choose the one that works for you.

1. Pour the sugar and hot or boiling water into a blender, and then blend until sugar is dissolved (about a minute).

2. Pour the sugar and hot or boiling water into a large jar or bottle and secure the lid, and then shake until sugar is dissolved (about a minute).
3. Bring the water to almost boiling in a pot, add the sugar, and then stir until dissolved.

Allow the syrup to cool and then store in bottles or jars in the refrigerator for up to a week. If you need to make more, then increase the portions. The sugar in this base recipe can be replaced with honey, agave, Splenda, maple syrup, brown sugar, or whatever you want.

Now, let us say, for example, that you want to make a ginger syrup. All you need to do is add hot ginger-flavored water with the sugar and you will have ginger syrup. To make ginger-flavored water, you would wash some gingerroot, cut it in slices, put it into a pot with water, and then bring to a boil. Once it starts to boil, turn it down to simmer for about thirty minutes so it extracts the ginger flavor from the gingerroot. When ready, strain out the ginger and then add your sugar to the ginger water. Mix until the sugar melts and voila! You made ginger syrup.

Now, let us say you want to make cucumber syrup. Well, cucumbers are more delicate than gingerroot, so you'll want to infuse sliced cucumbers with water in a jar and then let sit on the counter for a few hours. You can agitate the jar a few times to help the cucumbers release flavor faster. When finished, just strain the cucumber water into a pot and set on medium. For the sugar to melt, you will need to heat the cucumber water warm enough.

You now know how to make any simple syrup or any flavored simple syrup you want with any fruit, vegetable, spice, or herb. In addition, when making citrus syrup from lemons, limes, oranges, etc., you only use the rind of the fruit, not the meat.

Grenadine: Replace the water portion with pomegranate juice.

Tea Syrup: Add tea bags to the water when heating.

When you are ready for the next level, get creative and try combinations such as honey-ginger syrup, mint-agave syrup, cinnamon-orange syrup, jalapeño-maple syrup, etc.

MARGARITA MIX

Why use store-bought Margarita mix when you can make the real (and better) stuff at home? If you want to avoid sugar and need a low glycemic option, then try Markus Sweet, Monkfruit sweetener, stevia, or xylitol.

Makes 6 cups

- 2 cups fresh lime juice
- 2 cups simple syrup
- 2 cups water

Blend ingredients in a blender for ten seconds, or shake ingredients together in a large lidded jar, then stop and do a taste test. Some people like sweet mix and some like sour. Some like to add a little orange juice. Just adjust the amount of simple syrup, water, or lime juice according to your personal preference. This will keep in the refrigerator for two days and you can always freeze it.

SWEET-AND-SOUR MIX (OFTEN CALLED SOUR MIX)

The egg whites will put a nice frothy top on top of a Whiskey Sour. If you want to use the mix for a Rum Punch or Long Island Iced Tea, you can leave them out. If you want to avoid sugar and need a low glycemic option, try Markus Sweet, Monkfruit sweetener, stevia, or xylitol.

Makes 6 cups

- 2 cups fresh lemon juice
- 1/2 cup fresh lime juice
- 2 cups simple syrup
- 4 organic egg whites
- 1 cup water

Blend ingredients in a blender for ten seconds, or shake ingredients together in a large lidded jar, and then stop and do a taste test. Some people like sweet mix and some like sour. Just adjust the amount of simple syrup, water, or lemon juice according to your personal preference. With egg whites, it will only keep half a day. Without egg whites, it will keep two days and you can always freeze it.

PIÑA COLADA MIX

It is easy to make real Piña Colada mix, so there's no reason to buy the stuff on the shelf. You can find the Coco López in the mixer section of your local grocer.

Makes 10 cups

- 1 (46-ounce) can of pineapple juice (fresh-squeezed pineapple juice)

- 2 (15-ounce) cans of Coco López coconut cream
- 6 drops vanilla extract

Blend all the ingredients in a blender for five seconds, then refrigerate. It will last for two days and you can always freeze it.

STRAWBERRY DAIQUIRI MIX

You will thank yourself for taking the time to make your own strawberry mix. If you want to avoid sugar and need a low glycemic option, then try Markus Sweet, Monkfruit sweetener, stevia, or xylitol.

Makes 5 cups

- 2 cups unsweetened frozen strawberries, semi-thawed

- 1/2 cup fresh lime juice
- 1 cup simple syrup

Blend all the ingredients in a blender for about ten seconds. Stop, taste test, and then adjust the amount of simple syrup, lime juice, and strawberries according to your personal preference. Refrigerate. It will last for three days and you can always freeze it. If you want it to last two weeks, leave out the fresh lime juice and add to the blender when making a Strawberry Daiquiri or Margarita.

BAR PUNCH

Need something quick to make a Rum Punch without having to pick up five containers? Then just batch these ingredients together. If you need less, cut the recipe in half.

Makes 1 gallon

- 4 cups fresh-squeezed orange juice
- 4 cups pineapple juice
- 2 cup homemade grenadine
- 4 cups sweet-and-sour mix, without egg whites

Pour all ingredients into a gallon container. It will last for three days and you can always freeze it.

BLOODY MARY MIX

This recipe will get you started making your own Bloody Mary mix. You can adjust it to your own taste preferences. You can also add other ingredients such as roasted garlic, rosemary, basil, beef bouillon cubes, wasabi, avocado, apple cider vinegar, chili powder, and bitters.

Makes 1 gallon

- 2 ounces lime juice
- 8 ounces A.1. sauce
- 4 ounce raw horseradish (optional)
- 8 ounces Lea & Perrins Worcestershire sauce
- 1 heaping tablespoon black peppercorns, blended
- 1 heaping tablespoon celery seed, blended
- 2 (46-ounce) cans whole plum tomatoes
- Water as needed
- Dashes of Tabasco sauce, if desired

Add the lime juice, A.1. sauce, horseradish, and Worcestershire sauce into a large open-mouthed container. Pour the celery seed and peppercorns in a blender and blend on high for thirty seconds, and then dump into the large container. Fill the blender halfway with the whole plum tomatoes and then add water to fill.

Blend on high for twenty seconds. Fine-strain into the container. Continue this step until all the tomatoes have been blended and strained. Mix all ingredients, pour into sterilized jars or bottles, and refrigerate.

ROSE WATER

This recipe is for rose water, but you can use the petals of any nontoxic flower to make fragrant water.

Makes 1 cup

- 3 cups filtered water
- 2 cups rinsed rose petals

- 1 ounce vodka

Pour petals and the water into a pot, then bring to a boil. Simmer, covered, for thirty minutes. Cool, then strain into a sterilized container or bottle. Add vodka for preservation.

14

The Jewelry of the Drink: Cocktail Garnishes

Ask any girl and she will tell you that a cocktail garnish is the jewelry of the drink. Could you imagine a classic Martini served without an olive or a Manhattan without a cherry? It just would not be the same. Garnishes on cocktails were simple from the 1700s to the late 1990s, but when Martini bars popped up all over America between the late 1990s and the mid-2000s, they offered menus with 100+ flavored Martinis. Garnishes consisted of a lot of double-dipped rims of chocolate, caramel, honey, crushed candy, crumbled Oreos, flaked coconut, nuts, sprinkles, and more. This time period overlapped with the beginning of the craft cocktail movement, so the cocktail culture pendulum was swinging to both ends of the spectrum. You could compare it to the mid-1970s to the early 1980s music industry tension, when there were two groups of music lovers: fans of disco and those of rock 'n' roll.

Today, most of the frou-frou Martinis with store-bought mixers and cheap booze are gone, and there is always a new crazy garnish because it's fun. Since 2010 the craft cocktail culture has taken their well-thought-out elegant garnishes to a whole new level.

THE TOP FIVE EDIBLE COCKTAIL GARNISHES EVERY BAR HAS

1. Limes
2. Lemons
3. Olives
4. Cherries
5. Oranges

Cocktail garnishes can be anything edible such as fruit, vegetables, herbs, spices, flora, candy, baked goods, dairy, and even meat products. The only limit when it comes to garnishes is your imagination. Yes, there are common bar garnishes, but most bartenders like to experiment with new garnishes. Generally, the garnish is placed on top of a cocktail, but it can also be placed on the rim. The garnish flavor should always complement the flavor of the cocktail.

FRUIT GARNISHES

Olives are classified as a fruit because they are formed from the ovary of the flower. This particular fruit has the possibility of being stuffed. Most come already stuffed with a red pimento pepper. From the late 1990s to the mid-2000s, Vodka Martinis with blue cheese–stuffed olives were all the rage. Today, you can make your own stuffed olives. Stuffing ideas include cheese of your choice, roasted garlic, Italian sausage, nuts, jalapeño, pickled onion, pepperoni, or anchovies.

COMMON FRUIT GARNISHES

Apples, cherries, bananas, blackberries, blueberries, coconut, cucumbers, grapes, grapefruit, lemons, limes, watermelon, olives, oranges, pineapples, raspberries, and strawberries.

NOT SO COMMON FRUIT GARNISHES

Apricots, avocados, boysenberries, cranberries, dates, dragon fruit, figs, raisins, guava, kiwi, kumquat, lychee, mango, melon, nectarine, blood oranges, tangerine, papaya, passion fruit, peaches, pears, plums, star fruit, and tomatoes.

VEGETABLE GARNISHES

COMMON VEGETABLE GARNISHES

Celery, green onions, pearl onions, pickled beans, and pickled okra.

NOT SO COMMON VEGETABLE GARNISHES

Beets, ginger, and rhubarb.

HERB GARNISHES

COMMON HERB GARNISHES

Basil, chives, cilantro, dill, lavender, lemongrass, mint, rosemary, sage, and thyme.

NOT SO COMMON HERB GARNISHES

Borage, caraway, catnip, fennel, garlic, parsley, oregano, and tarragon.

SPICE GARNISHES

Spice garnishes can be mixed with salt or sugar and then put on the rim of the glass. They can also be sprinkled (or grated) on top of a cocktail that has a frothy head or on top of whipped cream. Some can be used in their whole form such as cinnamon sticks and star anise.

COMMON SPICE GARNISHES

Black pepper, cayenne, celery salt, chili powder, cloves, cinnamon, nutmeg, salt, star anise, and vanilla beans.

NOT SO COMMON SPICE GARNISHES

Ancho chili, anise seed, bay leaf, cumin, caraway seed, crystallized ginger, saffron, and white pepper.

FLORA GARNISHES

A Vanda orchid was first garnished a cocktail in Hawaii, by bar legend Harry Yee, in 1957. Since around 2005, bartenders have been searching for beautiful, nontoxic, edible flora to use in their cocktails. All common fruits, vegetables, and herbs go through a flowering stage, and all of these are nontoxic and safe to use. It's more important to know what flora is toxic and not safe to use as a garnish in your cocktail. For example, during the holiday season you may think that a sprig of mistletoe would be a perfect garnish for your holiday cocktail, but mistletoe is toxic. Always search the internet before using any questionable flora as a garnish.

NONTOXIC FLORA GARNISHES

Aloe Vera, angelica, orchids, daisy, dandelion, chamomile, chrysanthemum, clover, eucalyptus, forget-me-nots, gardenia, hibiscus, impatiens, jasmine, lavender, lilac, magnolia, marigold, orchid, pansy, peony, primrose, rose, snapdragon, sunflower, tulip petals (not the bulb), violet, water lily, and zinnia.

TOXIC FLORA GARNISHES

Angel's trumpet, azalea, belladonna (also called deadly nightshade), bird of paradise, bluebell, buttercup, calla lily, daffodil, English ivy, foxglove, hyacinth, hydrangea, iris, lily of the valley, lucky bamboo, mistletoe, morning glory, rhubarb leaves, star of Bethlehem, sweet pea, tobacco, tomato leaves, and wisteria.

CANDY AND BAKED GOODS GARNISHES

Garnishing with candy and baked goods (such as cookies) started in the late 1990s when the flavored Martini craze began. Before then, the sweetest cocktail garnish was a sugared rim. Because you have so many ingredients to choose from, this category of garnishes is totally up to your imagination. Here are some ideas: rock candy sticks, sugarcane sticks, chocolate-covered strawberries, Tootsie Pops, fortune cookies, a glazed doughnut set horizontally on the glass rim, gummy worms, licorice straws, marshmallows, Peeps, and placing a cookie horizontally on the rim and then poking a hole for a straw.

RIMMER GARNISH IDEAS

When rimming a glass at home, all you need is two plates. One plate will hold your dry garnish (salt, sugar, sprinkles, crushed cookies, etc.) and the other plate will hold the wet garnish that acts as a glue so the dry garnish can stick to the glass. Lemon or lime juice can be used for salts and sugars, but you will need something stickier to attach crushed cookies, sprinkles, etc. Some good choices include melted chocolate and syrups.

There are many flavored and colored sugar and salts that you can purchase, but you can also make your own at home. Sugar and salt are staples in the rimming world. For sugar you can use white, raw, brown, and powdered. If you want to color it, you just need some food coloring and plastic storage bags. When using salted rims on cocktails, you want to use a coarse kosher salt and not table salt. Sugar and salt can be combined with a myriad of spices and herbs to create a new flavor. Combinations might include cinnamon-sugar, cayenne-sugar, edible gold flake and sugar, dried cilantro and salt, cracked black pepper and salt, and dried basil and salt. As for crushing candy and cookies, double-bagging plastic storage bags and then banging the treats with a mallet until crushed is the best way.

Other rimming garnishes to try are sprinkles, Pop Rocks, flaked coconut, Cajun spices, edible pearl dust, chocolate powders, shaved chocolate, and crushed nuts.

DAIRY GARNISHES

The most popular dairy cocktail garnish is whipped cream. You can make your own whipped cream by whipping cream and sugar, or in a pinch you can pick up a can at your local grocery store. The most popular alcoholic drinks that use whipped cream are hot coffee, cider, and chocolate drinks.

BLOODY MARY GARNISHES

Since the 1970s the Bloody Mary has been the winner for the most edible garnishes of any cocktail in the world. Vintage Bloody Mary ads from the 1930s through the 1960s show very little garnishing for the Bloody Mary: one celery stalk, one lemon, and a lemon and celery stalk. The olive makes an appearance in the 1960s.

Bloody Mary garnishing from the 1970s through the 1990s included salted rims, Cajun spice rims, pickles, pickled beans, green onions, cherry tomatoes, peel-and-eat shrimp, oyster on the half shell, and blue cheese–stuffed olives.

In the 2000s, the Bloody Mary Bloody Bar was born. Vodka companies approached popular restaurants and bars offering free signage, menus, infusion jars, and, of course, a discount on their vodka. The establishment would set up a table filled with containers with a variety of garnishes, hot sauces, and mixes for guests to choose from. With time and for competition's sake, the garnish choices got more insane—well, insane for that time. Choices included beef jerky, hard bacon strips, Slim Jims, pizza-themed garnishes with rims of Parmesan cheese and pepper flakes, spaghetti-themed garnishes with meatballs, olive brine to make it dirty, an assortment of cheese cubes, and so much more.

Steve Schumacher's "Fried Chicken Bloody Mary" at Sobelman's Pub & Grill in Milwaukee, Wisconsin.
© *Steve Schumacher*

By 2012, the BM bars began to fade and a new, exaggerated Bloody Mary craze was born. Dave Sobelman from Sobelman's Pub & Grill in Milwaukee is given credit for the ultimate, most excessive, over-the-top Bloody Mary to date. He calls it a Chicken Fried Bloody Mary and it's garnished with a whole fried chicken.

Today, many bars are offering personalized Bloody Mary check-off menus. You are given a printed card and pen and you simply check off the items you want—choices such as vodka, rimming, and garnishes—for your Bloody Mary. Basically they are saving the time and trouble of setting up a table and keeping a small Bloody Mary bar behind the bar.

BLOODY MARY FRUIT GARNISHES

Cucumbers, lemons, limes, olives, and pineapple.

BLOODY MARY VEGETABLE GARNISHES

Asparagus, avocado, brussels sprouts, carrots, celery, baby corn, cocktail onions, fried onion rings, green onions, jalapeño poppers, mushrooms, peppers (all types), pickles (all types), pickled beans, pickled okra, radishes, and tomatoes (all types).

BLOODY MARY ANIMAL-BASED GARNISHES

Bacon, beef jerky, calamari, cheese (all kinds), cheeseburgers, cheesecake, chicken (all kinds; parts and whole), clams, cocktail sausages, crab, crawfish, fish (all kinds), ham, hot dogs, lobster, mac & cheese, meatballs, mussels, oysters, pepperoni, pizza (whole and sliced), ribs, salami, sandwiches (all kinds), shrimp, Slim Jim, and steak.

COCKTAIL DECORATIONS AND TOOLS

Probably the most iconic nonedible cocktail decoration is the paper parasol (also called the cocktail umbrella).

Cocktail decorations and tools mainly consist of pics (also called picks) and straws. Pics help hold an edible garnish near the top of your drink so it doesn't sink to the bottom, and straws help you sip the cocktail—if you choose not to drink from the rim—and also stir it up more if you desire.

Pics can come in sizes in length from three inches to twelve inches and they can be made of bamboo, wood, plastic, and metal. There are hundreds of pic designs in the world plus companies that specialize in creating logo picks.

Straws can come in sizes in length from five-and-a-half inches to eighteen inches. Most are made of plastic, but they can also be made of paper, bamboo, metal, and glass. Some can bend and some are fat.

Other popular nonedible decorations are little plastic animals and creatures that sit on the rim of your glass. These shapes include monkeys, mermaids, elephants, and giraffes. Lots of bars will have special decorations for signature drinks. For example, Tropical Isle in New Orleans has a drink called the Shark Attack that comes with a blue hollow plastic shark. The bartender pours grenadine (blood) inside the shark and then nose-dives it into your drink. Other decorations you may run across include a bamboo back scratcher, Krazy Straws, rim-hanging shot glasses, hot test tubes filled with booze and pushed into your drink, and indoor drink sparklers.

CRAZY COCKTAIL GARNISHES

Every day bartenders come up with new techniques for creating garnishes. International bartender competitions tend to have amazing, intricate, food-styled garnishes that replicate those of a five-star chef. Others are clever, experimental, or just plain over-the-top. Here are several examples to give you inspiration:

Lady's Leg Cosmopolitan from Eau de Vie in Sydney, Australia. © *Eau de Vie Sydney*

1. Eau de Vie—a craft bar in Sydney, Australia offers beautiful presentations for all their cocktails. One fun presentation is called "Lady's Leg," which is prepared in a vintage late-1930s cocktail shaker in the shape of a lady's leg complete with a high-heeled silver shoe. The cocktail uses a house-made cranberry sorbet instead of cranberry juice, giving the drink a creamy and soft texture. It is served in sexy vintage champagne coupes. View their stunning gallery of cocktails at eaudevie.com.au/sydney.

2. The Cocktail Professor team from Amsterdam has some of the best drink presentations and garnishes in the world (view their website, Facebook, and Instagram). Examples include an edible paper plane on a twisted classic Aviation cocktail; a twisted Old-Fashioned garnished with an edible wax seal; a cocktail served in a glass pipe that you can suck to drink and blow to blow bubbles; a cocktail with a small bag of pineapple caviar clipped on the rim with a mini clothespin; a cocktail with a swipe of white chocolate then torched coconut on the side of the glass as opposed to the rim; and several smoking cocktails.

3. At the Chicago tiki bar Three Dots and a Dash, the Treasure Chest (for eight) is a rummy drink served in and garnished with orchids, skulls, and other items one might see in a treasure chest.

4. The Black Ant in New York City serves a cocktail that is rimmed with salt and crushed black ants. The Mexican black ants are supposed to be an aphrodisiac. Oh, they also say that it pairs well with an order of Tlayuda con Chapulines, which are crunchy tortillas with sautéed grasshoppers.

5. Victor Tangos in Dallas serves a cocktail made with house-made oyster mushroom syrup and garnished with a candied shiitake mushroom.

6. Cassia in Santa Monica offers a cocktail that is garnished with a spoon of sea urchin roe.

7. In the London bar Nightjar, garnishes include a matcha green-tea cookie, an origami bird sprayed with perfume, and a dried starfish.

8. In New York City, Shigefumi Kabashima created a cocktail that sits in an ice-filled, skull-shaped glass and is garnished with a burning stick of sacred palo santo.

9. Canadian Frankie Solarik is a bar chef who is blowing minds with his garnish techniques. He says: "It's the idea of presenting a drink as a dish. I strive to compose cocktails with the same visual, visceral, and taste appeal, and complexity that is possible within a dish. The general goal for me artistically is to challenge the conventional thought as to what's possible within the medium of a glass." View his gallery on his website, and photos on Facebook, to grasp the beauty and inventiveness of his mind.

10. Lounge Bohemia in London created the Bubble Bath Martini. It's garnished with rose foam and a baby rubber ducky.

15

Cocktails 101: A Guide to Classic, Modern Classic, Popular, Famous, Official IBA, and Standard Cocktails

WHAT EXACTLY ARE THE DIFFERENCES BETWEEN A CLASSIC, MODERN CLASSIC, POPULAR, FAMOUS, OFFICIAL IBA, AND STANDARD COCKTAIL?

CLASSIC COCKTAIL

A "classic" cocktail has stood the test of time and is well known in cocktail culture around the world. They are generally classy and documented. Many come from cocktail recipe books from the 1880s through the 1940s, which were written by bartenders. Examples include the Martini, Manhattan, Mint Julep, and Old-Fashioned. Other vintage classics that may sound new to unseasoned bartenders include the Aviation, Blood and Sand, Clover Club, and Corpse Reviver.

MODERN CLASSIC COCKTAIL

A "modern classic" cocktail is a recent category—due to the cocktail revolution. It is a cocktail that has become a classic in modern time. As time passes, new categories will probably be added (that will more than likely be categorized by periods of time), but for now, it is safe to say that a modern classic could span between present time and back thirty years.

Modern classic cocktails can go viral as a result of media; however, that has not happened since the Cosmopolitan in 1999. Some can be discovered on cocktail menus that then attract the attention of the media. Good examples of this include the Benton's Old-Fashioned invented by New York City bartender Don Lee when he created a new spirit infusion technique he calls fat washing. He then made a bacon-flavored whiskey to use in his cocktail. Or when Portland bartender Jeffrey Morgenthaler barrel-aged a barrel of Negronis. These two are examples of doing something that has never been done before, but not all modern classic cocktails need be this way. They can be as simple as Paul Harrington's Jasmine or Dick Bradsell's Bramble. Modern classic cocktails can also come from winning competitions or from a menu that has won awards.

POPULAR COCKTAIL

A "popular" cocktail can be popular for a short period like a Toasted Almond from the 1980s, Purple Hooter from the 1990s, or Incredible Hulk from the 2000s, but if it remains popular for many years, it then becomes famous. It can be famous locally or globally. Locally famous cocktails include Detroit's Hummer, Alabama's Yellowhammer, and Maryland's Black-Eyed Susan. World-popular cocktails include the Piña Colada, Margarita, and Long Island Iced Tea.

OFFICIAL IBA COCKTAIL

An official IBA cocktail comes from the International Bartenders Association. The association was founded on February 24, 1951, in the Saloon of the Grand Hotel in Torquay, England. It is an international organization representing the best bartenders in the world and sanctions a list of official cocktails. The IBA has three categories of cocktails: The Unforgettables, Contemporary Classics, and New Era Drinks. The IBA categories will have some classics, modern classics, popular, famous, and standard cocktails.

STANDARD COCKTAIL

A "standard" cocktail is likened to a standard piece of music. All good musicians should be able to play many standards in many genres. Similarly, a good bartender anywhere should be able to make a standard cocktail or mixed drink. Mixed drinks are simple and often fall into the two-ingredient highball category such as a Screwdriver, Rum & Coke, Gin & Tonic, etc. There are standards in classic cocktails, popular cocktails, famous cocktails, and even official IBA cocktails categories.

TYPES OF COCKTAILS

In vintage cocktail books, types organized many cocktails. Bartenders who study these books still use these types as guidelines. Some bartenders will say that eleven types are too many and they can be condensed to four or five types:
- **Cobbler**—contains a spirit, sugar, and a garnish of fruits.
- **Collins**—contains a spirit, lemon juice, simple syrup, and carbonation.

- **Daisy**—contains a spirit, lemon juice, and a sweetener such as gum syrup, raspberry syrup, or grenadine.
- **Fix**—contains a spirit, lemon juice, and sugar, and is served with crushed ice.
- **Fizz**—like the Collins, it contains a spirit, lemon juice, sugar, and carbonation. Almost like a Sling.
- **Flip**—contains a spirit, egg, sugar, and spice (no cream).
- **Egg Nog**—contains a spirit, egg, sugar, spice, and cream.
- **Julep**—contains a spirit, sugar, and mint.
- **Punch**—started with containing five ingredients served in a large bowl for communal drinking: spirit, citrus juice, water, sugar, and spice.
- **Rickey**—contains a spirit, lime juice, and club soda.
- **Sling**—contains a spirit, lemon juice, sugar, and sometimes carbonation, and is served in a tall glass, almost like a Fizz.

COCKTAIL MAKING TIPS

PRE-CHILLING AND HEATING GLASSWARE

A cocktail glass needs to be chilled so it does not warm a shaken and strained cocktail. You can keep glasses in the freezer, or before you make the cocktail, place ice (or ice and water) into the cocktail glass so it will be chilled when you are ready to fill it. Simply discard the ice when necessary. Hot cocktails should be served in warmed (preheated) mugs for a similar yet opposite reason.

TOOLS

Tools needed: cocktail shaker (two-piece Boston or three-piece cobbler), mixing glass (or use the sixteen-ounce pint glass of the Boston shaker), jigger or jiggers (with measures for .25 ounce, .5 ounce, .75 ounce, 1 ounce, and 1.5 ounce), wide peeler for large citrus zests and peels, channel knife for thin zests and spirals, a sharp knife for cutting garnishes, Hawthorne strainer, a manual citrus squeezer, and assorted glassware.

TIN VS. GLASS

These recipes will instruct you to pour the ingredients into a shaker tin. This refers to a three-piece cobbler shaker tin because it is assumed that these cocktails will be made at home.

If making them behind a commercial bar, then you would add the ingredients to the sixteen-ounce pint mixing glass or second half of a Boston shaker.

INGREDIENTS

Juices

When a juice is called for in a recipe, it means fresh-squeezed juice. This particularly applies to lemon, lime, grapefruit, orange, and pineapple.

Cherries

Cherries for garnishing should be real (not clown-nose-red fake cherries). A good brand is Luxardo or use fresh cherries.

ALPHABETICAL RECIPE LIST OF CLASSIC, MODERN CLASSIC, POPULAR, FAMOUS, OFFICIAL IBA, AND STANDARD COCKTAILS

AMERICANO

Classic, popular, famous, IBA Unforgettable, and standard.

Add ice to a rocks glass or Old-Fashioned glass, then pour in:

- 1 ounce Campari
- 1 ounce sweet vermouth
- 1 ounce soda water

Gently stir, then garnish with an orange slice.

Gaspare Campari invented the Americano in the 1860s in his bar, Caffè Campari, in Milan, Italy. The name of the cocktail changed from Milano-Torino to Americano in the early 1900s when it became popular with American tourists.

Variation

Negroni: replace the soda water with gin.

AVIATION

Chill a cocktail glass, then pour the following into a shaker tin:

- 2 ounces gin
- .5 maraschino liqueur (like Luxardo)
- .5 ounce lemon juice
- .25 ounce crème de violette (like Rothman & Winter)

Add ice to the shaker tin and shake, then strain into the chilled cocktail glass. Garnish with a cherry.

BACARDI COCKTAIL

Classic and IBA Unforgettable.

Chill a cocktail glass, then pour the following into a shaker tin:

- 1.5 ounces Bacardi light rum
- 1 ounce lime juice
- 1 ounce grenadine

Add ice to the shaker tin and shake, then strain into the chilled cocktail glass. Garnish with a cherry.

In the early 1930s, Bacardi learned that New York bartenders were making the Bacardi Cocktail with other branded rums, so they took a case to New York's Supreme Court. In 1936, Justice John Walsh ruled that the Bacardi Cocktail must be made with Bacardi rum.

Variation

Daiquiri: replace the grenadine for simple syrup.

BELLINI

Famous and IBA Contemporary Classic.

Chill a champagne flute, then add the following:

- 4 ounces prosecco, cold
- 1.5 ounces fresh peach puree, cold

Stir gently.

Bartender and bar owner Giuseppe Cipriani (1900–1980) invented the Bellini in 1931 at his bar, Harry's Bar, which is located in Venice, Italy.

Variation

Puccini: replace the fresh peach puree with fresh mandarin juice.

Rossini: replace the fresh peach puree with fresh strawberry puree.

Tintoretto: replace the fresh peach puree with fresh pomegranate juice.

BETWEEN THE SHEETS

Classic and IBA Unforgettable.

Chill a cocktail glass, then pour the following into a shaker tin:

- 1 ounce Cognac
- 1 ounce white rum
- 1 ounce triple sec
- .75 ounce fresh lemon juice
- .25 ounce simple syrup

Add ice to the shaker tin and shake, then strain into the chilled cocktail glass. The Between the Sheets is believed to have been invented by Harry MacElhone at Harry's New York Bar in Paris, France, in the 1930s.

Variation

Side Car: omit the rum, replace the triple sec with Cointreau, and add a sugared rim.

BLACK RUSSIAN

Classic, popular, famous, IBA Contemporary Classic, classic, and standard.

Add ice to a rocks glass then pour in:

- 1 ounce vodka
- 1 ounce coffee liqueur

Stir gently.

It is believed that bartender Gustave Tops created the Black Russian in 1949 at the Hotel Metropole in the Belgian city of Brussels, for American socialite Perle Mesta (US Ambassador to Luxembourg).

White Russian: add 2 ounce cream.

Mississippi Mudslide: add 1 ounce cream and 1 ounce Irish cream.

Sombrero: omit the vodka and layer 1 ounce cream on top of the coffee liqueur.

Smith & Kerns/Kearns: replace the vodka with soda water and add 1 ounce cream.

Smith & Wesson: add 1 ounce cream and 1 ounce soda water.

Colorado Bulldog: add 1 ounce cream and 1 ounce cola. Often this drink is served in a tall glass and ingredient portions are raised.

Dirty Mother: replace the vodka for brandy.

Dirty White Mother: replace the vodka with brandy and add 1 ounce cream.

Toasted Almond: replace the vodka with amaretto and add 1 ounce cream.

Roasted Toasted Almond: add 1 ounce amaretto and 1 ounce cream.

Girl Scout Cookie: replace the vodka for white crème de menthe and add 1 ounce cream.

BLOODY MARY

Popular, IBA Contemporary Classic, and standard.

Add the following to a tall 12-ounce glass:

- 1.5 ounces vodka
- 5 ounces tomato juice
- .5 ounce lemon juice
- .5 ounce Worcestershire sauce
- Dash of Tabasco
- Celery salt and pepper to taste

Add ice gently, then stir. Garnish as you wish.

This recipe is from the IBA. If you make or purchase a Bloody Mary mix, then you would just combine the spirit and the mix. Who invented the Bloody Mary is not quite clear, but most believe it was either Fernand Petiot at Harry's New York Bar in Paris, France, or George Jessel in New York City. Both claimed they created the drink in the 1920s.

Variation

Bloody Maria: replace the vodka with tequila.

Bloody Caesar: add 3 ounces clam juice.

Red Snapper: replace the vodka with gin.

Bloody Joseph: replace the vodka with Scotch.

BLUE HAWAII

Famous.

Fill a 12-ounce Hurricane glass with ice, then add the following:

- .75 ounce vodka
- .75 ounce Puerto Rican rum
- .5 ounce blue Curaçao (preferably Bols)
- 1 ounce pineapple juice
- .5 fresh lemon juice
- .5 ounce simple syrup

Stir to mix and add water dilution. Garnish with pineapple slice and orchid and serve with aloha.

This is the exact recipe from the inventor, Harry K. Yee. Yee who invented the Blue Hawaii in 1957 at the Hawaiian Village on the island of O'ahu. Not to be confused with the Blue Hawaiian, which no one really knows the recipe for because it was made up by many trying to copy the Blue Hawaii.

Harry Yee at age ninety-eight in 2016 holding a Blue Hawaii from the Hilton Hawaiian Village where he created it in 1957. © *Dennis Oda*

BRAMBLE

Modern Classic and IBA New Era Drink.

- 2 ounces gin
- 1 ounce fresh lemon juice
- 1 ounce blackberry liqueur

Prepare an Old-Fashioned glass with crushed ice, then pour the first two ingredients into a shaker tin. Add ice to the shaker tin, shake then strain over the crushed ice, then gently stir. Pour the blackberry liqueur over the top of the drink in a circular fashion and garnish with a lemon slice and two blackberries.

Invented in the 1980s by bartender Dick Bradsell at Fred's Club in London, England.

BRANDY ALEXANDER

Classic, IBA Unforgettable, and standard.

Chill a cocktail glass, then pour the following into a shaker tin:

- 1 ounce Cognac
- 1 ounce fresh cream
- 1 ounce dark crème de cacao (white cacao can be used if you do not have dark)

Add ice to the shaker tin and shake, then strain into the chilled cocktail glass. Garnish with fresh grated nutmeg.

Variation

Alexander: replace the Cognac with gin.

Grasshopper: replace the Cognac with green crème de menthe and the dark cacao with white cacao.

Pink Squirrel: replace the Cognac with crème de noyaux and the dark cacao with white cacao.

Golden Cadillac: replace the Cognac with Galliano and the dark cacao with white cacao.

Banshee: replace the Cognac with banana liqueur and the dark cacao with white cacao.

BRANDY CRUSTA

Classic and famous.

Prep a small fancy 5-ounce wine glass (with a narrow diameter rim) by moistening the outside of the glass—near the rim—one inch in height with a lemon slice, then roll in granulated sugar. The result will be a one-inch band of sugar around the rim. Take a whole lemon and a wide peeler (or paring knife if you're skilled) and peel the entire rind off in one long piece. Coil the lemon rind the size of the diameter of your glass and place inside at the top. Some of the rind should be sticking up a little higher above the rim and be able to stay secured on its own. Pour the following into a shaker tin:

- 2 ounces Cognac or brandy
- .5 ounce lemon juice
- .5 ounce orange Curaçao
- 1 dash Angostura bitters

Add ice to the shaker tin and shake, then strain into the prepped glass. The Brandy Crusta is known as the first "fancy cocktail" and the first cocktail to use citrus juice. Joseph Santini in New Orleans invented it sometime in the early 1850s. The cocktail made it into the first known American cocktail recipe book, *How to Mix Drinks or The Bon-Vivant's Companion: The Bartender's Guide* by Jerry Thomas and precedes the Side Car and Lemon Drop Martini.

CABLE CAR

Modern classic.

Prep the rim garnish by adding a half-cup granulated sugar and one teaspoon of ground cinnamon into a plastic bag, shake to mix, then pour out on a saucer or plate. Run a lemon slice around the rim of a chilled cocktail glass, then dip into the cinnamon-sugar mixture. Pour the following into a shaker tin:

- 1.5 ounces Captain Morgan Spiced Rum
- .75 ounce Marie Brizard Orange Curaçao
- .5 ounce simple syrup
- 1 ounce lemon juice

Add ice to the shaker tin and shake, then strain into the chilled rimmed cocktail glass. Garnish with an orange spiral.

Invented in 1996 by craft cocktail pioneer Tony Abou-Ganim at the Starlight Room in San Francisco's Sir Drake Hotel.

CAIPIRINHA

Classic, popular, famous, and IBA Contemporary Classic.

Muddle half of a lime that is cut into two pieces and two teaspoons of granulated sugar in the bottom of a rocks glass or old-fashioned glass. Fill the glass with ice, then pour in the following:

- **2 ounces cachaça**

Stir to mix and to melt in a little water dilution in the drink.
This is Brazil's national drink.

CAPE CODDER

Popular and standard.

Add the following to a 10–12 ounce highball glass:

- **1.5 ounces vodka**
- **4 ounces cranberry juice**

Add ice, then garnish with a lime wedge.

Variation

Vodka Cranberry: omit the lime wedge.
Scarlett O'Hara: replace the vodka with Southern Comfort.
Sea Breeze: use equal parts cranberry and grapefruit juices.
Bay Breeze: use equal parts cranberry and pineapple juices and omit the lime wedge.
Woo Woo: add 1 ounce peach schnapps and adjust the vodka portion to 1 ounce.

CHAMPAGNE COCKTAIL

Classic, IBA Contemporary Classic, and standard.

Chill a champagne flute or coupe. Place a sugar cube on a palm-held napkin or into the bowl of a bar spoon, then dash 2–3 dashes of bitters onto the sugar cube. Drop the bitters-soaked cube into the chilled champagne glass, then add the following:

- **4 ounces chilled champagne.**

The first mention of the Champagne Cocktail was in 1855 in the book *Panama in 1855* by Robert Tomes. Tomes's version included ice and brandy. The next time it was seen in print was in the first American cocktail recipe book, *How to Mix Drinks* by Jerry Thomas, which included a lemon peel garnish and a small lump of ice. There have been slight variations of the cocktail over the years, but the one given is the most common.

CLOVER CLUB

Classic and IBA Unforgettable.

Chill a cocktail glass, then fill a shaker tin half full with ice and add:

- **2 ounces gin**
- **.75 ounce French dry vermouth**
- **.75 ounce raspberry syrup**
- **.75 ounce lemon juice**
- **1 egg white**

Shake well, then strain into the chilled glass.

Variation

Clover Leaf: add a spring of fresh mint when shaking, and then garnish with a mint sprig.

COSMOPOLITAN

Modern Classic, popular, famous, IBA Contemporary Classic, and standard.

The stories for each of the five Cosmopolitans can be found at misscharming.com's Cosmopolitan History page.

NEAL MURRAY'S COSMOPOLITAN

Pour the following into a shaker tin with ice:

- 1.5 ounces Gordon's vodka
- .75 ounce Leroux triple sec
- .75 ounce Rose's lime
- .5 ounce cranberry juice

Shake, then strain into a conical-shaped cocktail glass. Garnish with a lime wedge.

MELISSA HUFFSMITH-ROTH'S COSMOPOLITAN

Chill a conical-shaped cocktail glass, then pour the following into a shaker tin:
2 ounces Absolut Citron vodka

- 1 ounce Cointreau
- 1 ounce lime juice
- .5 ounce cranberry juice

Add ice to the shaker tin and vigorously shake, then strain into the chilled cocktail glass. Garnish with a lemon twist. Melissa says, " The color should be a pale ballet pink and cloudy from the fresh lime juice and ice—clean and refreshing like a pink lemonade for grownups.

TOBY CECCHINI'S COSMOPOLITAN

Chill a conical-shaped cocktail glass, then pour the following into a shaker tin:

- 1.5 ounces Absolut Citron vodka
- .75 ounce Cointreau
- .75 ounce lime juice
- .75 ounce cranberry juice

Add ice to the shaker tin and shake, then strain into the chilled cocktail glass. Garnish with a lemon twist. To be authentic, make an old-school lemon twist by cutting the ends off a lemon and then cutting halfway into the lemon lengthwise (not the circumference). Hull out the lemon meat with a spoon, so you are left with the whole rind. Roll up the rind, insert a toothpick (or bar pick) through the roll to secure, then cut slices to make curled lemon twists.

CHERYL COOK'S COSMOPOLITAN

Pour the following into a mixing glass filled with ice:

- 2 ounces Absolut Citron vodka
- .5 ounce triple sec
- .5 ounce Rose's lime
- .5 ounce cranberry juice

Stir, then strain into a conical-shaped cocktail glass. Garnish with a lemon twist. To be authentic, make this old-school lemon twist by cutting one end of a lemon then cutting about eight vertical incisions around the lemon. When needed, pull off a twist.

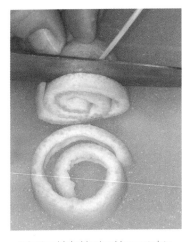

Toby Cecchini old school lemon twists.
© *Cheryl Charming*

Cheryl Cook old school lemon twists.
© *Cheryl Charming*

DALE "KING COCKTAIL" DEGROFF'S COSMOPOLITAN

This recipe is from DeGroff's 2002 book, *The Craft of the Cocktail*. Originally, the vodka he used was Absolut Citron and the triple sec was Cointreau.

Chill a conical-shaped cocktail glass, then pour the following into a shaker tin:

- 1.5 ounces Ketel One Citron vodka
- .5 ounce triple sec
- .25 ounce lime juice
- 1 ounce cranberry juice

Add ice to the shaker tin and shake, then strain into the chilled cocktail glass. Garnish with a flamed orange zest.

CUBA LIBRE

Popular, IBA Contemporary Classic, and standard.

Add the following to a 10-ounce highball glass:

- 1.5 ounces light rum (preferably Cuban)
- 4 ounces Cola

Add ice, then garnish with a lime wedge.

Variation

Rum & Coke: omit the lime wedge.

DAIQUIRI

Classic, popular, famous, IBA Unforgettable, and standard.

Chill a cocktail glass, then pour the following into a shaker tin:

- 1.5 ounces light rum
- 1.5 ounces simple syrup
- 1 ounce lime juice

Add ice to the shaker tin and shake, then strain into the chilled cocktail glass.

DARK 'N STORMY

Popular, Famous, IBA New Era Drink, and standard.

Add the following to a tall 12-ounce glass:

- 1.5 ounces Gosling's Black Seal rum
- 5 ounces ginger beer

Add ice, then garnish with a lime wedge.

DEATH IN THE AFTERNOON

Popular, Famous, IBA New Era Drink, and standard.

Chill a champagne flute, then add the following:

- 4 ounces dry champagne, cold
- 1 ounce absinthe (like Lucid)

Gently stir. Some will not find this sweet enough; so if you desire, you can add simple syrup or a sugar cube to taste.

ESPRESSO MARTINI

IBA New Era Drink

Chill a cocktail glass, then pour the following into a shaker tin:

- 1.5 ounces premium vodka
- .5 ounce simple syrup
- 1 ounce Kahlúa coffee liqueur
- 1 shot strong espresso

Add ice to the shaker tin and shake, then strain into the chilled cocktail glass. Garnish with three coffee or espresso beans in the center to resemble flower petals. Invented by Dick Bradsell at London's Fred's Club in the late 1980s. Bradsell made it at the request of an up-and-coming model, Kate Moss, who wanted a cocktail that could both wake her up and mess her up.

FRENCH 75

Classic, popular, famous, IBA Contemporary Classic, and standard.

Chill a champagne flute, then add the first ingredient. Pour the last three ingredients into a shaker tin:

- 4 ounce dry champagne, cold
- 1 ounce Cognac
- .5 ounce simple syrup
- .5 ounce lemon juice

Add ice to the shaker tin and shake, then strain on top of the champagne and then garnish with a lemon twist.

Variation

French 75 (British style): replace the Cognac with gin.
French 76: replace the Cognac with vodka.

GODFATHER

Classic, IBA Contemporary Classic, and standard

Add ice to a rocks glass or an Old-Fashioned glass, then pour in:

- 1.5 ounces Scotch
- 1.5 ounces amaretto

Stir gently.

Variation

Godmother: replace the Scotch with vodka
French Connection: replace the Scotch with Cognac

GRASSHOPPER

Classic, popular, famous, IBA Contemporary Classic, standard.

Chill a cocktail glass, then pour the following into a shaker tin:

- 1 ounce white crème de cacao
- 1 ounce green crème de menthe
- 1 ounce cream or half-and-half

Add ice to the shaker tin and shake for 10 seconds, then strain into the chilled cocktail glass.

HEMINGWAY DAIQUIRI

Classic and IBA Contemporary Classic.

Chill a cocktail glass, then pour the following into a shaker tin:

- 2 ounces light rum (preferably Cuban)
- .25 ounce maraschino liqueur
- .25 ounce simple syrup
- .75 ounce grapefruit juice
- .5 ounce lime juice

Add ice to the shaker tin and shake, then strain into the chilled cocktail glass. Garnish with a floating lime wheel if desired.

HURRICANE

Popular and famous.

Add the following to a large 22-ounce Hurricane glass:

- 2 ounces light rum
- 2 ounces gold or dark rum
- 1 ounce lime juice
- 1.5 ounces red passion fruit syrup (like Monin)
- 4 ounces orange juice

Add ice, stir, and add more ice if needed, then garnish with an orange slice and cherry.

It is believed that Pat O'Brien invented the Hurricane in 1942 in New Orleans. Sadly, today if you order one at Pat O' Brien's in New Orleans you will get a mass-produced red Kool-Aid-type drink. If you only have a 16-ounce Hurricane glass, then cut the portion of the rum to 1.5 ounces each.

IRISH COFFEE

Popular, famous, IBA Contemporary Classic, and standard.

- 1.5 ounces Irish whiskey
- 1 ounce simple syrup
- 5 ounces hot coffee
- 2 ounce cream float

Warm an 8-10 ounce coffee glass, then add the first three ingredients. Float the cream on top.

The Buena Vista Café in San Francisco makes 2,000 Irish Coffees a day. In 2008, they were entered into the Guinness Book of Records for making the largest Irish Coffee.

JACK ROSE

Classic.

Chill a cocktail glass, then pour the following into a shaker tin:

- 2 ounces Laird's applejack
- .5 ounce lemon juice
- .5 ounce lime juice
- .5 ounce handmade grenadine

Add ice to the shaker tin and shake, then strain into the chilled cocktail glass. Some claim this cocktail is made with lemon juice while others say lime, so this recipe covers both. Laird & Company (lairdandcompany.com) has been making applejack (apple brandy) since the 1600s and is the oldest distillery in America. President George Washington wrote the family a letter asking for the recipe and President Abraham Lincoln sold it in his saloon. Today, ninth generation Lisa Laird is the face of Laird & Company—the first woman to hold this position.

Lisa Laird, the ninth-generation owner of the oldest distillery in America, Laird & Company. © *Lisa Laird*

JASMINE

Modern Classic.

Chill a cocktail glass, then pour the following into a shaker tin:

- 1.5 ounces gin
- .75 ounce lemon juice
- .25 ounce Campari
- .25 ounce Cointreau

Add ice to the shaker tin and shake, then strain into the chilled cocktail glass. Garnish with a lemon twist.

Cocktail godfather Paul Harrington invented the Jasmine in the early 1990s. It was named after his roommate's last name. Years later he learned that the roommate spelled his last name without the "e" on the end.

KIR

Classic and IBA Contemporary Classic.

Chill a champagne flute, then add the following:

- 4 ounces dry white wine, cold
- 1 ounce crème de cassis (black currant liqueur)

Variation

Kir Royale: replace the wine with dry champagne.
Cardinal: replace the white wine with red wine.
Kir Impérial: replace the cassis with raspberry liqueur.
The Kir (rhymes with ear) is named after the French Mayor Felix Kir (1876–1968) of Dijon in Burgundy.

LEMON DROP MARTINI

Modern Classic, popular, and standard.

Rim a chilled cocktail glass with sugar, then pour the following into a shaker tin:

- 1.5 ounces lemon vodka
- 1 ounce triple sec

- 1 ounce lemon juice
- .5 ounce simple syrup

Add ice to the shaker tin and shake, then strain into the chilled rimmed cocktail glass, and then garnish with a lemon twist.

Variation

Flavored Lemon Drop Martini: replace the lemon vodka with other flavored vodkas.

LAST WORD

Modern classic and popular.

Chill a cocktail glass, then pour the following into a shaker tin:
- 1 ounce gin
- 1 ounce green Chartreuse
- 1 ounce maraschino liqueur (like Luxardo)
- 1 ounce lime juice

Add ice to the shaker tin and shake, then strain into the chilled cocktail glass. The Last Word is believed to have been invented by a bartender from Detroit, Michigan, named Frank Foggerty.

LONG ISLAND ICED TEA

Popular, famous, IBA Contemporary Classic, and standard.

- .5 ounce vodka
- .5 ounce gin
- .5 ounce light rum
- .5 ounce blanco tequila
- .5 ounce triple sec
- 1 ounce simple syrup
- 1 ounce lemon juice
- 1 ounce cola

Fill a 12–14 ounce tall glass with ice, then add the first seven ingredients. Top with more ice, add the cola, and then garnish with a lemon wedge.

Variation

Long Beach Tea: replace the cola with cranberry juice.
Miami Tea: replace the cola with Sprite and the triple sec with blue Curaçao.

MAI TAI

Popular, famous, IBA Contemporary Classic, and standard.

Add ice to an old-fashioned glass, then pour the following into a shaker tin:

- 1 ounce Rhum Clément VSOP Martinique rum
- 1 ounce Appleton Estate Extra dark Jamaican rum
- .5 ounce orange Curaçao
- .5 ounce orgeat syrup
- 1 ounce lime juice
- .25 ounce simple syrup

Add ice to the shaker tin and shake, then strain over the glass of ice. Garnish with a half-spent lime shell and mint sprig.

The Mai Tai is Tahitian for "out of this world," which translates to "very good." Vic Bergeron a.k.a. Trader Vic invented it in 1944. This recipe is from Jeff "Beachbum" Berry. In 1944, the recipe called for seventeen-year-old J. Wray & Nephew rum, but it is extinct. Beachbum says these rums will make it taste like the original Mai Tai.

MARGARITA

Classic, popular, famous, IBA Contemporary Classic, and standard.

Chill a cocktail glass, then pour the following into a shaker tin:

- 1.5 ounces tequila
- .5 ounce Cointreau (or triple sec)
- .75 ounce lime juice
- .75 ounce simple syrup

Add ice to the shaker tin and shake, then strain into the chilled cocktail glass. Garnish with a lime. If you desire salt, then you can prep the glass with a rim of coarse kosher salt. In addition, if you would like it on the rocks, then strain over an old-fashioned glass filled with ice.

No one knows who invented the Margarita, but there are several who claim to. It is, however, Mexico's national cocktail.

Variation

Golden Grand Margarita: use gold-colored/aged tequila and Grand Marnier in place of the Cointreau.

Blue Margarita: substitute blue Curaçao for the Cointreau.

MARTINI

Classic, popular, famous, IBA New Era Drink, and standard.

Chill a cocktail glass, then pour the following into a mixing glass:

- 2 ounces London dry gin
- 1 ounce French dry vermouth

Add ice to the mixing glass and stir, then strain into the chilled cocktail glass. Garnish with a green olive, lemon twist, or both.

Variation

Vodka Martini: replace the gin with vodka and shake instead of stir.

Dirty Martini: add 1 ounce olive brine.

Dry Martini: use half the amount of vermouth.

Very Dry Martini: omit the vermouth.

Perfect Martini: use equal parts dry and sweet vermouth.

Gibson: garnish with a pickled cocktail onion.

Bronx: a Perfect Martini with 1 ounce orange juice added.

Burnt Martini: a splash of Scotch is added.

Dry Martini Cocktail from William Boothby in 1907: equal parts gin and vermouth and a dash of orange bitters.

No one knows who invented the Martini. There are several stories and varied recipes, but that is all we have.

MANHATTAN

Classic, popular, famous, IBA Unforgettable, and standard.

Chill a cocktail glass, then pour the following into a mixing glass:

- 2 ounces rye whiskey
- 1 dash Angostura bitters
- 1 ounce sweet vermouth

Add ice to the mixing glass, then stir and strain into the chilled cocktail glass. Garnish with a cherry.

Variation

Rob Roy: replace the rye whiskey with Scotch whisky.

MIMOSA

Classic, popular, IBA Contemporary Classic, and standard.

Chill a champagne flute, then add the following:

- 4 ounces champagne
- 2 ounces orange juice

Garnish with an orange slice or orange twist or strawberry.
A Buck's Fizz and a Mimosa are the same drink.

MINT JULEP

Classic, popular, IBA Contemporary Classic, and standard.

- Drop four mint sprigs into the bottom of an 8-ounce stainless-steel julep cup or highball glass and gently tap with a muddler to release the oils. Fill the glass with cracked ice, then add the following:
- 2 ounces Bourbon whiskey
- 1 ounce simple syrup

The Mint Julep is one of America's oldest cocktails, dating back to the late 1700s when it was made without ice.

MOJITO

Classic, popular, famous, IBA Contemporary Classic, and standard.

Drop two mint sprigs (about 10 leaves) into the bottom of a tall 12-ounce glass and gently tap with a muddler to release the oils. Then add the following:

- 2 ounce light rum (Cuban preferably)
- 1 ounce lime juice
- 1 ounce simple syrup
- 3 ounces soda water

Add ice, stir gently, then garnish with a mint sprig.
A medicinal version of this drink for sailors was first mentioned in 1586. The first known time it was seen in print with these exact five ingredients was in Havana's Sloppy Joe's 1936 *Cocktails Manual.*

1

2

4

5

1. Vesper. © *Wollertz / Shutterstock*

2. Modern Sidecar. © *Brent Hofacker / Shutterstock*

3. Mint Julep. © *Brent Hofacker / Shutterstock*

3

6

4. Clover Club Cocktail. © Elena Demyanko / Shutterstock

5. Sazerac. © Brent Hofacker / Shutterstock

6. Classic Margarita. © Brent Hofacker / Shutterstock

MONKEY GLAND

Classic and IBA Unforgettable.

Chill a cocktail glass, then pour the following into a shaker tin:

- 2 ounces gin
- 1.5 ounces orange juice
- .25 ounce absinthe
- .25 ounce grenadine

Add ice to the shaker tin and shake, then strain into the chilled cocktail glass. Garnish with an orange zest. For more absinthe aroma, keep absinthe in a small spray bottle, omit the absinthe in the recipe, then spray over the top of the finished cocktail.

Invented in Paris by either bartender Frank Meier or Harry MacElhone in 1923. The name comes from a famous doctor of the time who believed that grafting monkey gland (testicle) tissue onto human males would provide longevity and rejuvenation.

MOSCOW MULE

Classic, popular, IBA Contemporary Classic, and standard.

Add the following to a 12-ounce copper cup or old-fashioned glass:

- 1.5 ounces Smirnoff vodka
- 5 ounces ginger beer

Add ice, then garnish with a lime wedge.

Variation

Dark 'n Stormy: replace the vodka with Gosling's Black Seal Rum.

Kentucky Mule: replace the vodka with Kentucky Bourbon.

Tennessee Mule: replace the vodka with Tennessee whiskey.

Mexican Mule: replace the vodka with tequila.

Irish Mule: replace the vodka with Irish whiskey.

Scottish Mule: replace the vodka with Scotch whisky.

Kentucky Mule: replace the vodka with Bourbon.

Ginger Mule: replace the vodka with gin.

Chilcano: replace the vodka with pisco.

The Moscow Mule is America's first vodka drink that introduced Smirnoff vodka.

NEGRONI

Classic, popular, famous, IBA Unforgettable, and standard.

Add ice to a rocks glass or old-fashioned glass, then pour in:

- 1 ounce gin
- 1 ounce Campari
- 1 ounce sweet vermouth

Gently stir, then garnish with an orange slice or twist.

Variation

Americano: replace the gin with soda water.

OLD-FASHIONED

Classic, popular, IBA Unforgettable, and standard.

- Drop a sugar cube into the bottom of an Old-Fashioned glass, dash with four dashes of Angostura bitters, then add .25 ounce of water. With a muddler, crush the sugar cube, and stir with the muddler until dissolved. Add the following:
- 2 ounces Bourbon or rye whiskey

Drop in a chunk of ice (preferably one you've picked from a block of ice), then add an orange zest. In the "old" days, they would icepick off chunks from blocks of delivered pond ice. You can make your own ice chunks by filling a metal baking pan with water, or by cutting off the tops of dairy (and nondairy) paper containers, cleaning them, then filling them with water and freezing.

Variation

The original Old-Fashioned (late 1700s–early 1800s): omit the ice chunk, replace the orange twist with a lemon twist, and serve with a small spoon in the glass. The spoon always stays in the glass.

Old-Fashioned in the mid to late 1800s: replace the orange twist with a lemon twist.

Wisconsin Old-Fashioned: replace the whiskey with brandy, muddle an orange wedge and cherry, replace the sugar cube with 1 ounce simple syrup, fill the glass with ice, stir and garnish with an orange wedge and cherry.

PIÑA COLADA

Classic, popular, famous, IBA Contemporary Classic, and standard.

Pour the following into a blender:

- 1.5 ounces light rum (preferably Puerto Rican)
- 3 ounces pineapple juice
- 1 ounce Coco López coconut cream

Add a half-cup of ice, then blend for 10 seconds. Pour into a poco grande glass (or glass of your choice) and garnish with a pineapple wedge and cherry. The Piña Colada is Puerto Rico's national cocktail.

Variation

Bushwhacker: replace the light rum with dark rum and add 1 ounce coffee liqueur.
Bahama Mama: add 1 ounce orange juice, .5 ounce lime juice, and .5 ounce grenadine (basically a marriage between a Rum Punch and a Piña Colada).
Miami Vice: layered half Piña Colada and half Strawberry Daiquiri.
Painkiller: add 1 ounce orange juice and grate fresh nutmeg on top.

PISCO SOUR

Classic, famous, IBA New Era Drink, and standard.

Chill a cocktail glass then pour the following into a shaker tin:

- 1.5 ounces pisco
- .75 ounce simple syrup
- 1 ounce lime juice
- 1 egg white, raw

Add ice to the shaker tin and shake, then strain into the chilled cocktail glass. Garnish with three dashes of Angostura bitters on top.
The Pisco Sour is Peru's national cocktail.

RAMOS GIN FIZZ

Classic, famous, and IBA Unforgettable.

Chill an 8-ounce juice glass, then pour the following into a shaker tin:

- 1.5 ounces Old Tom gin
- .5 ounce lemon juice
- .5 ounce lime juice
- 1 ounce simple syrup
- 1 ounce heavy cream
- 1 small egg white
- 1 dash orange-flower water

Add a half-cup of ice to the shaker tin and shake for five minutes. Add 1 ounce soda water to the chilled glass, then strain cocktail into the chilled glass to the top. Charles Ramos created the Ramos Gin Fizz in 1888 at his New Orleans bar, the Imperial Cabinet. It is believed that he employed a line of "shaker boys" to shake and pass down the cocktail in an assembly line.

RUSTY NAIL

Classic, popular, IBA Unforgettable, and standard.

Add ice to a rocks glass or Old-Fashioned glass then pour in:

- 2 ounces Scotch whisky
- 1 ounce Drambuie

Gently stir, then garnish with a lemon twist.

SAZERAC

Classic, popular, famous, IBA Unforgettable, and standard.

Set out two Old-Fashioned glasses and chill one by adding ice and water into it. In the second glass add a sugar cube, .5 ounce of water, and 4 dashes of Peychaud's (PAY-showds) bitters—it must be Peychaud's. With a muddler, crush the sugar cube, and stir with the muddler until dissolved. Add the following:

- 2 ounces rye whiskey

Add ice, then stir with a bar spoon. Empty the first glass chilling with iced water, then add .25 ounce of absinthe and swirl inside the glass to coat. Strain the mixture from the second glass into the first glass, then garnish with a lemon twist. You can keep absinthe in a small spray bottle and spray the inside of the glass if so desired. You can also use .5 ounce simple syrup in place of the sugar cube and water.

It is said that this preparation method was the original way the Sazerac was made. Today, you can skip the second old-fashioned glass and just use a mixing glass. The Sazerac has been New Orleans's official cocktail since 2008.

SCREWDRIVER

Popular, IBA Unforgettable, and standard.

Add ice to an Old-Fashioned or highball glass, then pour in:

- 1.5 ounces vodka
- 5 ounces orange juice

Garnish with an orange wedge.

In 1959, the *Washington Post* published, "It was in Ankara during World War II that a group of American fliers invented a drink called the 'Screwdriver'—orange juice and vodka—because they couldn't stand Turkish vodka. This was a slur on Ankara's estimable cuisine which at its worst is never so dreadful as the Screwdriver."

Variation

Madras: use equal parts orange and cranberry juices.

Fuzzy Navel: replace the vodka with peach schnapps.

Hairy Navel: add 1 ounce peach schnapps.

Sex on the Beach: add 1 ounce peach schnapps to the Madras.

Harvey Wallbanger: float 1 ounce Galliano on top.

Melon Ball: add 1 ounce melon liqueur.

Alabama Slammer: add .5 ounce sloe gin, .5 ounce Southern Comfort, and .5 ounce amaretto.

SEA BREEZE

Popular, IBA Contemporary Classic, and standard.

Add ice to an Old-Fashioned or highball glass, then pour in:

- 1.5 ounces vodka
- 2.5 ounces grapefruit juice
- 2.5 ounces cranberry juice

Add ice then garnish with a lime wedge.

SEX ON THE BEACH

Popular, IBA Contemporary Classic, and standard.

Add ice to an Old-Fashioned or highball glass, then pour in:
- 1 ounce vodka
- 1 ounce peach schnapps
- 2.5 ounces cranberry juice
- 2.5 ounces orange juice

Garnish with an orange wedge.

SIDECAR

Classic, Famous, IBA Unforgettable, and standard

Chill a cocktail glass, then pour the following into a shaker tin:
- 2 ounces Cognac
- 1 ounce Cointreau
- 1 ounce lemon juice

Add ice to the shaker tin and shake, then strain into the chilled cocktail glass.

Variation

Modern Sidecar: add a sugared rim.

SINGAPORE SLING

Classic, famous, and IBA Contemporary Classic.

Add ice to a tall 16-ounce glass (or Hurricane glass) then pour the following into a shaker tin:
- 2 ounces gin
- 1 ounce cherry brandy or Cherry Heering

- .5 ounce Cointreau
- .5 ounce Bénédictine
- 3 ounces pineapple juice
- 1 ounce lime juice
- 1 dash Angostura bitters

Add ice to the shaker tin and shake for two seconds, then strain over the ice. Garnish with a pineapple slice and cherry.

It is claimed that the Singapore Sling was invented at the Raffles Hotel in Singapore. It is believed that the original recipe was lost, but these are the ingredients known today.

STINGER

Classic, IBA Unforgettable, and standard.

Chill a cocktail glass, then pour the following into a shaker tin:
- 2 ounces brandy
- 1 ounce white crème de menthe

Add ice to the shaker tin and shake, then strain into the chilled cocktail glass.

Variation

Vodka Stinger: replace the brandy with vodka.

TEQUILA SUNRISE

Popular, Famous, IBA Contemporary Classic, and standard.

Add the following to a tall 12-ounce glass:
- 1.5 ounces tequila
- 5 ounces orange juice

Add ice, then pour in 1 ounce grenadine. It will sink to the bottom creating a gradient (sunrise) effect. Garnish with orange slice and cherry.

Variation

Tequila Sunset: replace the grenadine with blackberry brandy.
Caribbean Sunrise: replace the tequila with rum.
Vodka Sunrise: replace the tequila with vodka.

The Tequila Sunrise was invented by Bobby Lozoff in 1969 at the Trident in Sausalito, California.

TOMMY'S MARGARITA

Modern classic and IBA New Era Drink.

Chill a cocktail glass, then pour the following into a shaker tin:
- 2 ounces reposado tequila
- 1.5 ounces lime juice
- .75 ounce agave nectar

Add ice to the shaker tin and shake, then strain into the chilled cocktail glass. Created by Julio Bermejo at Tommy's Mexican Restaurant in San Francisco in the early 1990s.

VESPER

Famous, and IBA New Era Drink.

Chill a cocktail glass, then pour the following into a shaker tin:
- 3 ounces Gordon's gin
- 1 ounce Smirnoff vodka
- .5 ounce Cocchi Americano

Add ice to the shaker tin and shake, then strain into the chilled cocktail glass. Garnish with a large thin slice of lemon peel.

The Vesper is a fictional cocktail first seen in Ian Fleming's 1953 novel *Casino Royale*. It is named after Bond's love interest. In the casino, Bond asks for "three measures of Gordon's, one of vodka, half a measure of Kina Lillet. Shake it very well until it's ice-cold, then add a large thin slice of lemon peel. Got it?" Kina Lillet is extinct, so the closest substitute is Cocchi Americano.

VIEUX CARRÉ

Classic and famous.

Add ice to an Old-Fashioned glass, then pour in:

- 1 ounce rye whiskey
- 1 ounce Cognac
- 1 ounce sweet vermouth
- .25 ounce Bénédictine
- 2 dashes Peychaud's Bitters
- 2 dashes Angostura bitters

Gently stir, add more ice if needed, then garnish with a lemon twist.

The Vieux Carré (VOO- ka-RAY) translates into "old square," which means the French Quarter where it was invented by head bartender Walter Bergeron at the Carousel Bar in the Hotel Monteleone in 1934.

WHISKEY SOUR

Classic, popular, IBA Unforgettable, and standard.

Add ice to an Old-Fashioned glass then pour the following into a shaker tin:

- 1.5 ounces Bourbon whiskey
- 1 ounce simple syrup
- 1 ounce lemon juice
- 1 egg white

Add ice to the shaker tin and hard shake for 30 seconds, then strain over the ice. Garnish with half orange slice and cherry. This cocktail can be served up in a cocktail glass as well.

Variation

Amaretto Sour: replace the Bourbon with amaretto.

Vodka Sour: replace the Bourbon with vodka.

Scotch Sour: replace the Bourbon with Scotch.

Apricot Sour: replace the Bourbon with apricot brandy.

Midori Sour: replace the Bourbon with Midori melon liqueur.

WHITE LADY

Classic and IBA Unforgettable.

Chill a cocktail glass, then pour the following into a shaker tin:

- 2 ounces gin
- .5 ounce Cointreau
- .5 ounce lemon juice
- 1 egg white

Add ice to the shaker tin and shake, then strain into the chilled cocktail glass.

Invented by bartender Harry MacElhone at Ciro's Club in London, then revamped to this recipe ten years later at Harry's Bar in Paris.

ZOMBIE

Famous.

Pour the following into a blender:

- 1.5 ounces gold Puerto Rican rum
- 1.5 ounces dark Jamaican rum
- 1 ounce 151-proof Lemon Hart Demerara rum
- .75 ounce fresh lime juice
- .5 ounce Falernum
- 1 teaspoon grenadine
- 6 drops Pernod
- 1 dash of Angostura bitters
- .5 ounce Don's mix (2 parts grapefruit juice to 1 part cinnamon-infused sugar syrup)
- Add 3/4 cup of small ice and blend for 5 seconds, then pour into a tiki mug or tall glass.

Add ice to fill, then garnish with a mint sprig.

Don the Beachcomber created the Zombie at his bar in Hollywood in 1934.

16

Serving Cocktails: A Guide to Cocktail Vessels

A BRIEF HISTORY OF DRINKING VESSELS

The first drinking vessels were made of pottery, wood, metals—or in a pinch—objects such as a cracked coconut shells, animal horns, etc.

The first "glass" was made naturally from black volcanic glass. It is believed that starting around 2000 BCE, the people of Mesopotamia (now Northern Syria and Iraq) would melt volcanic glass, and then pour it into molds to make objects such as bowls and beads. The Romans improved on this idea around 50 BCE by sticking a molten glob on the end of a hollow tube and then blowing it into a shape. By the 1400s, glassmaking techniques greatly advanced. In the 1600s, and especially the 1700s, elegant glassware was found in most homes.

In the early 1800s, barkeeps only had about five types of bar glasses. By the end of the century, the first-rate bars had a glass for everything, sometimes totaling twenty-five types of bar glasses.

BASIC COCKTAIL GLASSWARE

A glass is the first thing you or a bartender will grab before making a cocktail. Now, of course, you can drink a Mai Tai from a recycled pickle jar, but if you live in the civilized world, you will want to drink cocktails in their proper glassware. At home, you can get away with delicate cocktail glassware, but in most bars you will find more durable glassware for obvious reasons.

From left to right: highball, rocks, Old-Fashioned, Double Old-Fashioned, Collins, shot, brandy snifter, champagne flute, champagne saucer/coupe, champagne trumpet, champagne tulip, cocktail coupe, cocktail conical, cordial, Hurricane, Irish coffee, Margarita, poco grande, punch cup, sherry, and tiki mug.

STURDY GLASSWARE

Highball
Seven to nine ounces. Most bars do not stock real highball glasses and just use short Old-Fashioned glasses, calling them highballs. Vintage films from the 1930s through the 1950s often show what is considered a highball glass.

Rocks
Around five to eight ounces and used for shooters and, of course, drinks on the rocks such as one-spirit (normally whiskey) or two-spirit drinks like a Rusty Nail or Black Russian.

Old-Fashioned
A nine-to-twelve-ounce, short, stocky glass, making it perfect for a highball such as a Scotch & Water, Gin & Tonic or—of course—an Old-Fashioned. Sometimes it is called a lowball glass.

Double Old-Fashioned
A twelve-to-fourteen-ounce, short, sturdy glass that is a little bigger than an Old-Fashioned glass. People who do not like the awkwardness of a tall glass will like these. It is also called a bucket glass.

Collins

A ten-to-twelve-ounce glass (also called a chimney glass) that is tall and thin with straight sides.

Shot

One-and-a-half-to-two-ounce short glass designed for shots of liquor.

STEMMED GLASSWARE

Brandy Snifter

Snifters can be found in sizes five to twenty-four ounces. They are used for brandy or Cognac; however, many spirits can be served in a snifter, including Sambuca (don't forget the three coffee beans), Grand Marnier, a fine tequila, a single malt Scotch, etc. Some bars like to use snifters for Brandy Alexanders and Milk Punches.

Champagne Flute

This will be a six-ounce glass (for a five-ounce pour) for champagne and champagne drinks.

Champagne Saucer/Coupe

A six-ounce glass for champagne and champagne drinks.

Champagne Trumpet

A six-ounce glass for champagne and champagne drinks that is a type of flute. It is tall and V-shaped like a trumpet.

Champagne Tulip

A six-ounce glass for champagne and champagne drinks that is a type of a flute. It has a curvy shape.

Cocktail Glass/Coupe

Cocktail coupes can range from five to ten ounces in size. Vintage coupes are on the small side, while modern coupes will be a little larger.

Cocktail Glass / Conical

These conical-shaped cocktail glasses are often referred to as a Martini glass. They range in sizes six to twelve ounces. Large Martini glasses are meant for cocktails that have mixers added to them.

Cordial

A cordial glass will be a small glass holding up to two ounces.

Hurricane

A twelve-to-twenty-two-ounce hurricane lamp–shaped glass that is used for tropical drinks.

Irish Coffee

A seven-to-ten-ounce glass mug used for hot drinks, or the traditional version, which is a stemmed glass without a handle (the latter is used at the Buena Vista Cafe where they make 2,000 Irish Coffees a day). If you use a larger mug at home, you will need to double up the booze to compensate for the extra size.

Margarita

A Margarita glass has a sombrero-shaped coupe and is between fourteen and sixteen ounces. There are other Margarita glasses with green cactus stems and glasses made of thick, bubbled Mexican glass.

Poco Grande

A Poco Grande glass is a short version of a Hurricane glass. It will be around fourteen ounces, and some bars will use this glass for all their tropical drinks, including Margaritas.

Punch Cup

A punch cup will be around six to eight ounces because punch is meant to be strong and served without ice in the cup.

Sherry

A four-to-five-ounce glass used for sherry and ports. A proper serving is three ounces.

Wine

Wineglasses can be seven to twenty-four ounces. Most bars carry one all-purpose wineglass used for both red and white wines, but "wine bars" will generally use large bowl glasses for reds and slender glasses for white. A proper pour of wine is six ounces; however, some bars will pour five ounces because they want to get five glasses out of a bottle.

NOVELTY

Coconut
The best way to make coconut cups for glassware is to use a band saw to saw off the top quarter part of the coconut and leave in the coconut meat.

Pineapple
Cut the top part of a pineapple off, then hull out the meat. To make hulling easier, invest in a pineapple corer.

Tiki
Tiki mugs come in a variety of shapes and sizes up to twenty-four ounces.

FUN COCKTAIL GLASSWARE FACTS

- In 1884, the G. Winter Brewing Company in New York published a bartender guide listing over twenty-five types of glassware that first-rate saloons should have.
- It has been said that the stemmed coupe glass was modeled after Marie Antoinette's bosom; however, this cannot be true because the glass was invented almost one hundred years before she was born.
- The twelve-ounce conical Martini glass was not created until the late 1990s when the flavored Martini craze happened. Glass producers had to make them larger so the added mixers could fit in the glass.
- The sixteen-ounce pint glass is the most popular all-purpose glass because it can be used for beer, a mixing glass, water, the second half of a Boston shaker, and tall (and double tall) drinks such as Long Island Iced Teas, lemonades, tropical drinks, Bloody Marys, and many more.
- On January 25, 2008, the world's largest champagne fountain was created with 43,680 glasses at the Shopping Center Wijnegem in Belgium.

17

Tools of the Trade: The Essential Cocktail Bar Tools

A BRIEF HISTORY OF COCKTAIL TOOLS

All professions have tools, and in the cocktail world, one bartender stands out on the subject of bar tools: Jerry "Professor" Thomas. Thomas published the very first American cocktail recipe book in 1862, and it is well known that he traveled the world with a set of solid silver bar tools. In the late 1700s to early 1800s, bar tools included punch bowls, silver ladles, citrus reamers and strainers, knives, nutmeg graters, spoons, small wineglasses for measuring, large containers to be used as measuring cups, pestles and mortars, sugar loaf nibs, and a muddler. In the late 1800s, bar tools began to be improved and patented.

BASIC BAR TOOLS

From left to right: barspoon, bottle opener, citrus squeezer, corkscrew, grater (microplane), jigger, muddler, Boston shaker, cobbler shaker, Hawthorne strainer, julep strainer, mesh strainer, wide peeler, zester/channel knife.

Only a few tools are needed to make great cocktails and, in a pinch, you can even find substitutes in your kitchen drawers. Sure, you can shake up a cocktail in a lidded Mason jar and strain it through your fingers, but if you want to get serious about cocktail making, then invest in a few tools.

BARSPOON

A barspoon has a long handle and you use it to stir cocktails, layer shots, spoon dry goods like sugar, and guide a thick frozen/blended drink out from the blender pitcher into a glass. Popular cocktails that require stirring include Gin Martinis, Manhattans, and Sazeracs.

To stir a cocktail, add your ingredients into a mixing glass and then add ice. Place the handle of the spoon between your middle and ring fingers, then insert the spoon to the inside of the mixing glass (bowl of the spoon touching the inside of the glass). Keep the bowl on the inside of the glass as you stir around. Twenty revolutions is a good stir.

All alcohols have different weights (densities), and when you layer a shot, you start with the heaviest alcohol on the bottom and the lightest on top. Let us say you want to layer Irish cream on top of coffee liqueur. Simply fill half of the shot glass with coffee liqueur, set the edge of the spoon bowl on top of the coffee liqueur level, and gently pour the Irish cream on the bowl (breaking the fall) so that it gently layers on top of the coffee liqueur. Some bartenders like to use the curved side of the bowl and others like the concave side of the bowl.

BOTTLE OPENER

A bottle opener opens bottles. There are many to choose from. They come in all colors and styles, with retractable reels, belt hooks, and so much more.

CITRUS SQUEEZER

A citrus squeezer squeezes citrus juice, and there are electric, manual, and handheld squeezers to choose from.

CORKSCREW

A corkscrew is also called a wine tool and used to open bottles of wine, stubborn corks on whiskey bottles, and as bottle openers. Many types are available, but real bartenders and wine stewards use a waiter's corkscrew. The best to buy is a "double lever" waiter's corkscrew, which comes with a small built-in knife to cut the foil off a wine bottle, but you will find the knife can serve many other purposes.

GRATER

A grater (microplane) is used mostly to grate fresh spices. Just hold the small, stainless-steel grater over the drink and grate. The most popular drinks that require nutmeg grating include Milk Punch and a Brandy Alexander.

JIGGER

A two-sided measurement tool to measure alcohol for cocktails. They come in about five different sizes. But if you can only buy two, get 1–2 ounce and 1.5–.5 ounce jiggers.

MUDDLER

A muddler is used to crush and mash fruits, sugar cubes, herbs, and more. Never use a varnished or lacquered muddler because those poisons will get into the drink. There are several muddlers to choose from today.

SHAKER TIN

A shaker is used to shake a drink. You can find novelty shakers in many shapes, but they all break down into two types: cobbler and Boston.

Cobbler shakers consist of three pieces and are mostly used by home enthusiasts. A Boston-type shaker consists of two components pieced together to shake a drink—normally a sixteen-ounce mixing pint glass and a twenty-eight-ounce shaker tin.

STRAINER

A strainer keeps ice and other ingredients that have been shaken from falling into the glass. Bartenders today use three types of strainers: Hawthorne, julep, and mesh.

Hawthorne strainers have a metal coil and can be used on top of a shaker tin or a mixing glass. Julep strainers fit at an angle into a mixing glass. A mesh strainer is used as a "double strainer"—meaning that it's held over the glass and used as a second strainer while pouring into the glass from a Boston or julep strainer. It makes sure seeds or small bits are caught before going into the drink.

WIDE PEELER

This is a peeler much like you have at home to peel vegetables but wider to cut citrus rinds.

ZESTER/CHANNEL KNIFE

These cut curly, fancy citrus twists.

THE BEST BAR TOOLS

Every profession has different grades and levels of tools—and bar tools are no exception. A one-stop shop for the leading high-quality bar tools is cocktailkingdom.com. There is also thebostonshaker.com, babsupplies.com, and the master mixology section of barproducts.com.

FUN BAR TOOL FACTS

› In the early cocktail-making days, sherry glasses were used as jiggers. It is also known that eggcups were often used as a jigger. Eggcups were mainly used for breakfast; a soft-boiled egg was placed into the cup, then cracked with a butter knife and eaten out of the shell with a spoon.

› The julep strainer was originally called an ice spoon.

› The barspoon is believed to come from apothecary medicine and pestle spoons.

› In 1932, popular jewelry company Napier produced a silver cocktail shaker with engraved recipes called "Tells-You-How Mixer." The engraved recipes included Alexander, Bacardi, Between the Sheets, Bronx, Clover Club, Dry Martini, Dubonnet, Gin Rickey, Manhattan, Old-Fashioned, Orange Blossom, Pam Beach, Sidecar, and Tom Collins. Initially, it was only sold at Saks Fifth Avenue. Today, you can buy one for around $1,200. Napier went on to produce many more cocktail shakers.

› The muddler was first called a toddy stick and was made of silver or hardwood.

› Double straining (straining with a Hawthorne and mesh strainer held over the cocktail glass) was first done by using a Hawthorne strainer and julep strainer held over the glass.

› To heat cocktails, vintage bartenders would plunge hot iron pokers from the fireplace into drinks. They were either called flip dogs or loggerheads.

› In 1850, the first known published illustration of a two-piece cocktail shaker was seen in the *London News*.

› To authentically strain a cocktail that is stirred in a mixing glass, you should leave the spoon in as you strain.

› In 1868, articles on American cocktails and cocktail shakers were published in two British publications: the British periodical *Notes and Queries* and *Meliora: A Quarterly Review of Social Science*.

- "This endeavor to get up a system of stimulation has given rise in America to the manufacture of 'cocktail' (a compound of whiskey, brandy, or champagne, bitters, and ice), dexterously mixed in tall silver mugs made for the purpose, called 'cocktail shakers.'"—*Notes and Queries*

- "They toss the drinks about; they throw brimful glasses over their heads; they shake the saccharine, glacial and alcoholic ingredients in their long tin tubes."—*Meliora: A Quarterly Review of Social Science*

- E. J. Hauck from Brooklyn, New York, patented a three-piece cocktail shaker in 1884.

- In 1889, a man from Connecticut created a metal spring to go around a strainer, and a few years later, the Connecticut company Manning & Bowman improved it and punched holes in it to read "Hawthorne," which was named after the Hawthorne Café in Boston.

- In 1892, Chicago bartender Cornelius Dungan patented the double cone jigger.

Neat or Straight Up: Getting Familiar with Drink-Making Terms

DRINK-MAKING TERMINOLOGY

- **Blend:** to mix up ingredients in an electric blender with ice. In America, generally the South says "frozen" and the North says "blended."
- **Build:** fill a glass with large ice and pour in the ingredients. If you have small, thin ice, pour your ingredients in first and then add the ice to avoid a lot of dilution.
- **Chill:** to chill a glass, add ice and then water to the glass and allow it to chill while you are making the drink. Alternatively, keep glasses chilled in the freezer.
- **Float:** gently pour a spirit on top of a drink.
- **Muddle:** to mash up ingredients with a muddler. Crush hard for ingredients like pineapple, citrus, ginger, etc. Softly tap herbs just to release the oils.
- **Neat:** room-temperature-pour straight from the bottle. No ice.
- **On the Rocks:** over ice.
- **Rim:** to add something to the rim of the glass.
- **Roll:** to roll a drink back and forth.
- **Shake:** to shake a cocktail with ice with a cocktail shaker.
- **Strain:** after shaking, strain the cocktail with a strainer.
- **Stir:** pour ingredients into a mixing glass; add ice, and then stir.
- **Straight Up:** a drink that is chilled by shaking or stirring then served cold straight up.

Rules to Drink By: Bar Etiquette

Every profession in the world could list ten things they want you to know. Dentists wish women wouldn't wear lipstick to appointments; off-duty doctors wish you wouldn't ask questions about your aches and pains; and supermarket cashiers wish you would take items out of the basket instead of sitting it on the belt.

The Top Ten Things Bartenders Want You to Know

1. Cash tips are king. It is common in America to be paid bimonthly, so bartenders have to wait two weeks to get their taxed credit card tips. Cash tips are king because it gives the bartender a little spending cash.

2. If a bartender asks you for a valid ID, take it as a compliment. There is a small window in life where you get to be young and beautiful, so enjoy it! Bartenders don't enjoy taking time to check your ID because it slows them down, but they have to follow state laws and work policies in order to keep their jobs.

3. Bartenders lose money if not tipped. Let us say that you do not tip on your $10 drink. The sale of that drink is still reported to the government and then taxed eight percent. The tax is taken out of their hourly pay. So, a $6 an hour bartender job can very quickly turn into a $1 an hour job. It is common for a bartender to not get a check at all.

4. Asking for a drink in a tall glass or with less ice does not mean you get more alcohol. It only means that you get your drink served in a tall glass with extra mixer. A drink with less ice means normal portions of alcohol and mixer with less ice. If you want more alcohol, then you will need to order a double.

5. Be respectful and leave the bar when it closes. Last call is normally given one half-hour before closing, and lights come up when it's closing time. Bartenders have another two hours cashing out, doing paperwork, stocking, cleaning, and hauling out trash before they can go home, so don't add extra time for them.

6. When you say, "Hook me up! Make my drink strong! Make it a good one!" what bartenders hear is, "Hey, I know we don't know each other and you could get fired, but will you please steal some booze for me?" Bars are a store and bartenders are the salespeople. They sell products owned by

other people, and therefore cannot give away things that are not theirs. A person who takes things that are not theirs is called a thief. Yes, some bar owners allow a small comp tab, but bartenders use it with discretion and for valid comps—not to steal something for you.

7. Most jobs are either physical or mental. Bartending is both. Bartenders spend their first two hours setting up the bar for the day and their last two hours closing down. Sandwiched in between they are remembering ten things in their head at all times (names, prices, drink orders, tabs, cocktail recipes, etc.), making many five-second decisions (whether you are of age, too intoxicated, safe, etc.), dealing with many personality types, and having to bend, reach, squat, and lift. It's physically and mentally draining.

8. Please do not announce, "I'm a bartender" or "I used to be a bartender" because real bartenders would never say that. Bartenders know you are in the biz by your actions.

9. Please stop handing over multiple cards to split your tabs when the bar is busy. If you insist on paying separately, then begin separate tabs at the beginning or do the best thing by taking turns buying rounds.

10. It is not the bartender's responsibility to charge and take care of your media devices. Bring your charge cord and we will be happy to let you know where the outlets are located. On the media note: please do not push your cell phone in bar staff faces with a cocktail recipe that has more than four ingredients.

HONORABLE MENTION

Stop being ripped off by lazy bartenders who do not give you the alcohol that you paid for.

Example #1: You order four chilled Patrón Silver shots. When the bartender shakes the tequila with ice (to chill it), water melts into the tequila. All four shots will not fit into four shot glasses now, so make sure you tell the bartender you want all the extra. You paid for it, so you deserve it.

Example #2: You order a frozen drink and the bartender makes it by hand in a blender. Everything in that blender is yours, so do not let them pour the finished drink into a glass, then have some leftover in the blender. You need to ask for the leftover because you've paid for that alcohol.

HOW TO ORDER A COCKTAIL AT A BAR

1.   When a bar is busy, always have your order/orders ready when the bartender approaches you. If you have questions or want to have a conversation about cocktails and choices, then let the bartender know so they can fit in the time needed to do that into their flow. The bartender may set you up with a few ideas and menu to give you a little time, then get back with you. Bartenders want to give you good service, but they also want to give everyone good service. If the bar is slow, then the bartender will be able to spend more time with you.

2.   When you know what you want, name the liquor first and your mixer second. Also, "call" your liquor (meaning to call out the brand you want). Examples include: Grey Goose & Cranberry, Jack & Coke, Bombay & Tonic, Ketel One Screwdriver, Knob Creek Rye Old-Fashioned, and Malibu & Pineapple.

3.   Well drinks. These are also called rail or house drinks. They are the least expensive mixed drinks. When you ask for a Gin & Tonic, then the bartender is using the cheapest gin to make your drink. However, a lot of corporate bars require the bartender to up sell, so the bartender will ask you if there is a gin you prefer or if you want your favorite gin used, etc. If you truly want the cheapest Gin & Tonic, then help the bartender by asking for a well Gin & Tonic. This eliminates a lot a time and monotony for the bartender.

4.   When ordering drinks that require details, always give the details. Examples include: Herradura Reposado Margarita on the rocks with salt; Bombay Sapphire Martini straight up, stirred with an olive and a twist; Belvedere Vodka Martini straight up, shaken with a twist; Double Glenlivet 12, neat with a water back; Hendrick's Negroni with Aperol up; and Jim Beam Rye Manhattan on the rocks. ("Up" is short for straight up. Straight up means that it has been chilled—shaken with ice—then strained into the glass. "Neat" means that it is poured out of the bottle at room temperature.)

5.   While the bartender is making your cocktail/cocktails, start getting your money ready. If you want to start a tab, then get your credit card ready. After delivering your cocktail, the next step for a bartender is to secure a transaction. Many have cameras on them and they are required to follow through with the transaction process.

Here are some common things people say to bartenders and ways to do and say them better.

You: What's good? Surprise me!

It is great that you want to try something new, but please narrow it down. First, we do not know what flavors, spirits, and types of cocktails you like or dislike. Second, we do not know if you are lactose intolerant, allergic to nuts, or have any dietary concerns. We also do not know what you are in the mood for. Are you celebrating something? Do you want something hot, boozy, refreshing, fruity, creamy, classic, etc.? Better ways to ask the bartender include:

- "I like vodka-based drinks with fruity flavors. I also love the taste of ginger, chocolate, or mint. Can you make me something tall and refreshing?"
- "Can you make me something off the top of your head? I'm game for anything. The only spirit I do not like is tequila and the only other flavor I do not like is licorice. I'd like something boozy on the rocks."
- "I'm celebrating! Can you make me something historic made with champagne?"
- "I had a craft cocktail in New York City that had a spicy liqueur in it that I really liked. Could you make me something spicy with Bourbon?"

You: Can I get a beer?

I know they do this in the movies, but it doesn't work in bars. Ask for a beer menu or ask the bartender where you can find the beer menu. Most bars offer many beers.

You: Can we get three shots of tequila?

Yes, you can, but what kind of tequila do you want? Do you want salt? Do you want limes? Ways to order shots of tequila include:

- "Can we get three shots of Patrón Silver with salt and limes?"
- "We need three chilled shots of Don Julio Reposado with limes."
- "We'd like to get three shots of well tequila with no salt or limes."

TRENDING: WHAT INFLUENCES OUR IMBIBING

MEDIA INFLUENCE ON COCKTAILS

Media. Is. Communication. It can be spoken, written, or broadcasted on radio, in newspapers, magazines, film, advertising, music, TV, internet, etc. Media can influence voters, the products you buy, your attitude, and a sense of what is or is not important to you. It always reflects and creates culture. It is powerful. So, if you think you don't know the name of a hit TV show featuring a New York City pink Martini being drunk by four attractive female friends—you're wrong. You know the name of the show—don't you? Media is even more powerful in today's world because of the speed of technology. Humans started with the spoken word, which led to cave paintings, smoke signals, handwriting, carrier pigeon, printing press, Morse code, typewriter, radio, vinyl albums, telephone, TV, word processor, cassette tapes, VHS tapes, compact discs, computers, internet, and social networking. Cell phones have become such an integral part of our everyday life that when watching a film or TV show from the 1990s, we often catch ourselves wondering for a few seconds, "Why don't they just call!...oh, it was the nineties."

INFLUENTIAL COCKTAIL MEDIA IN FILM

1934–1947 *THE THIN MAN*

The Thin Man (1934), *After the Thin Man* (1936), *Another Thin Man* (1939), *Shadow of the Thin Man* (1941), 1944 *The Thin Man Goes Home* (1944), and *Song of the Thin Man* (1947).

The *Thin Man* movies are without a doubt the most prolific series of films that highlight cocktails. Actually, it is the only film series. The series are comedic mystery films starring William Powell and Myrna Loy as Nick and Nora Charles. Nick is a retired private detective and Nora is a wealth heiress. Their imbibing cocktails of choice include a Martini, Knickerbocker, Bronx, gin, rye whiskey, and more.

1962 *DR. NO*

The first James Bond film is responsible for jumpstarting the sale of vodka in America—Smirnoff in particular. Before then, most Americans drank whiskey, brandy, rum, and gin. But when Sean Connery made his own Smirnoff Martinis in his hotel room and later ordered Vodka Martinis—shaken-not-stirred—it created a worldwide Vodka Martini frenzy. To date, vodka (still) is the number-one spirit sold in America.

1988 *COCKTAIL*

Many films have bar scenes, but when Tom Cruise introduced the entertainment-starved world to "Flair Bartending," it sparked a sensation. To this day, bar guests will still mention Tom Cruise anytime a bartender makes any kind of fancy movement. Many will ask, "Can you bartend like Tom Cruise?" TGI Fridays began to train their bartenders to perform fancy moves called "flair" in the late 1970s and 1980s. The word probably came from the pieces of flair—an assortment of extra fun pins stuck on server and bartenders suspenders—that the staff was required to wear. "Magic" Mike Werner, a Texas TGI Friday's bartender and trainer, is credited with planting the flair seed when he was flipping bottles around for fun. Werner was the first stacked domino, pushed to create a flair bartending chain reaction. TGI Friday's was the first to host a flair bartending competition, 1986's TGI Friday's Bar Olympics in Woodland Hills, California. The winner of the competition was John "JB" Bandy (Werner won second place). In 1987, Bandy was approached by Touchstone Pictures to be the flair bartending choreographer and bartender trainer for Tom Cruise and Bryan Brown for the 1988 film *Cocktail*. Many drinks were made, seen, and mentioned in the film, but most importantly, it kickstarted the flair bartending phenomenon.

2002 *DIE ANOTHER DAY*

Forty years after skyrocketing the Vodka Martini in 1962, James Bond (played by Pierce Brosnan) did it again—this time with a Mojito. The Mojito is a 1920s classic Cuban cocktail, but brand-new to audiences watching an orange bikini-clad Halle Berry rise from the water, walk to the bar, and have James Bond hand her a Mojito. Ever heard the term "overnight sensation"? Bar guests walked into bars ordering Mojitos and bartenders had zero fresh mint, or zero knowledge of this cocktail. The Mojito is still going strong.

2011 *CRAZY, STUPID, LOVE*

The 1800s Old-Fashioned was made popular again by the hit TV series *Mad Men* (2007–2015), so when charming movie star Ryan Gosling made Old-Fashioneds for himself and Emma Stone in 2011, it threw gas on the fire. Gosling learned his Old-Fashioned–making skills from superstar bartender Eric Alperin, co-owner of the esteemed Los Angeles craft bar Varnish. Today, it is one of the top cocktails men will order.

INFLUENTIAL COCKTAIL MEDIA IN MUSIC

1945 "RUM AND COCA-COLA," THE ANDREWS SISTERS

The Andrews Sisters in 1945. © *Photofest*

In 1943, this song was a hit in Trinidad. The song was stolen (don't worry, the owner got his day in court), its lyrics revamped, and then introduced to the Andrews Sisters.

It became the number-one song in America. Network radio stations banned it because it mentioned an alcoholic beverage and a brand (Coca-Cola). There were still a lot of dry states in America at the time, but history has proven one thing: when something is banned, it makes it more popular. The demand for the record was phenomenal. Decca Records sold seven million copies. Now, if we only knew the rum and the Coca-Cola sales, because the guess is that it was nothing short of mind-blowing.

1973 "TEQUILA SUNRISE," THE EAGLES

The recipe for a successful Tequila Sunrise:
- 1 cup Bartender Bobby Lozoff inventing it, then making one for Mick Jagger.
- 1 cup Mick Jagger asking for it at bars all over America while on tour.
- 1 cup Jose Cuervo putting the recipe on the back of their bottle in early 1973.
- Stir in a hit song by the Eagles and release it to the masses.

Bartenders from 1973 say that as soon as the song hit the airwaves customers were asking for the drink.

1977 "MARGARITAVILLE," JIMMY BUFFETT

Margaritas had been popular since the 1950s, but when Jimmy Buffett rose to the number-on spot on the charts with the song "Margaritaville," the drink was in high demand in bars everywhere. To meet the demand, bars stocked bottles of fake Margarita mixers. Today, many bars have gone back to using fresh-squeezed lime juice—thank you!

1979 "ESCAPE," RUPERT HOLMES

If you like Piña Coladas and getting caught in the rain, then you will like this song, but ask any bartender from 1979 their least favorite drink to make and they will say—yep!—Piña Colada. And it's all because of Rupert Holmes. Again, to keep up with the demand, the shelves were filled with fake Piña Colada mixers.

1993 "GIN & JUICE," SNOOP DOGG

Unbelievably, gin was not on the drinking radar at this time, so when Snoop Dog's second hit reached the Top Ten, bar guests began asking for it. Most did not understand what they were ordering—they just heard it on a hit song and wanted it. Bartenders were constantly asking, "What kind of juice would you like?" Seagram's reported that their sales shot to over three million cases that year and up to four million through the late 1990s. Soon, Seagram's began making flavored gin.

2001 "PASS THE COURVOISIER," BUSTA RHYMES AND P. DIDDY

Cognac had been mentioned in 1990s rap songs previously, but "Pass the Courvoisier" changed the genre of Cognac overnight. Thoughts of Cognac used to conjure images of men sitting in overstuffed leather chairs smoking cigars and drinking Cognac. This was a game-changer. On NPR in 2009, Courvoisier's marketing manager, Jennifer Szersnovicz, said, "It was huge for the brand and our volumes skyrocketed."

Some previous rap songs with Cognac or a brand of Cognac in their songs:
- 1990 "Humpty Dance," Digital Underground
- 1993 "Gz Up, Hoes Down," Snoop Dogg
- 1994 "The Genesis," Nas
- 1994 "Down for Whatever," Ice Cube
- 1994 "So Much Pain," TuPac
- 1996 "Nas Is Coming," Nas
- 1999 "Next Episode," DRE and Snoop Dog

In 2007, Snoop Dogg was approached by Landy Cognac to put their brand in a rap song. Now, that is the way to do it! One year later, Dogg released the Christmas rap song "Landy in My Eggnog."

INFLUENTIAL COCKTAIL MEDIA ON TV

1998–2004 SEX AND THE CITY

The very first episode showed Carrie and Samantha drinking Cosmopolitans at Miranda's birthday dinner; however the average viewer would not have known the cocktails were called Cosmopolitans. But on Sunday night, July 19, 1998, in season one episode seven, the cocktail was finally written into the transcript by Darren Star. The voice-over of character Carrie Bradshaw read: "That afternoon I dragged my poor, tortured soul out to lunch with Stanford Blach and attempted to stun it senseless with Cosmopolitans." And the rest is history.

Out of six seasons and 94 episodes, the Cosmopolitan was seen 27 times and mentioned by name four times. In 1999, season two most definitely set the Cosmopolitan tone for the rest of the seasons because the cocktail was seen in ten episodes and mentioned by name in three.

2006 THE OPRAH WINFREY SHOW

The *Oprah* show could make someone famous overnight. Any product mentioned skyrocketed in sales, and the same is true for cocktails. In 2006, Oprah Winfrey and Rachael Ray made Lemon Drop Martinis and Pomegranate Martinis. Lemon Drop shot and shooters had been around in the late 1980s and 1990s, but when the "Martini Bar" craze started (late 1990s–mid-2000s), it was common to see Lemon Drop Martinis, so bartenders could easily make it. The Pomegranate Martini was a different story. Bars did not carry pomegranate-flavored anything (juice, flavored liquor, syrup, or liqueur). Of course, as you might imagine, everyone started asking bartenders for Pomegranate Martinis the very same day the show aired. This is when POM brand pomegranate juice began to appear in the grocery stores.

Jon Hamm as Don Draper in *Mad Men*, 2009. © *AMC / Photofest*

Mad Men made many vintage cocktails from the late 1950s and the 1960s cool again. The Old-Fashioned is probably the most popular, but it was nice for bartenders to have twenty-somethings (millions turn twenty-one every day) order cocktails that their grandmothers or grandfathers might have ordered in their youth.

INFLUENTIAL COCKTAIL MEDIA IN PRINT

1905 ABSINTHE DRIP

Absinthe Drip had been enjoyed from the late 1700s, but in 1905, a global absinthe ban made it even more popular. International newspaper headlines in 1905 told the story about a Swiss farmer named Jean Lanfray who drank absinthe and then murdered his wife and daughters. To be fair, the media failed to mention the other alcohol he consumed that day, which included crème de menthe, Cognac, coffee with brandy, six glasses of wine with lunch, a glass of wine before leaving work, and then more wine after. America banned absinthe in 1912 and lifted the ban in 2007. Soon it began popping up in films such as *Moulin Rouge*, *Alfie*, and *Eurotrip*. Absinthe became a mystery, and once bar guests learned that it had been banned for ninety-seven years, they grew more intrigued.

1953 *CASINO ROYALE BY IAN FLEMING*

In the seventh chapter of Ian Fleming's first James Bond novel he created a fictional cocktail that lives on today—Vesper. As far as we know, it is the first time that gin and vodka had been mixed together in a cocktail. Bond requests his order be served in a deep champagne goblet and use three measures of Gordon's, one of vodka, and half a measure of Kina Lillet. Shake it very well until it's ice-cold, then add a large, thin slice of lemon peel.

A used 1995 postage stamp from the UK depicting Casino Royale. © *AMC / Photofest*

Acknowledgments

This book is part of a thirty-eight-year collection of cocktail history and trivia. It started with me scribbling bar tricks and magic on cocktail napkins; it then quickly grew in the 1980s–1990s when I was able to meet thousands of tourists tending bar on a Caribbean cruise ship and at Walt Disney World. Its next growth spurt started when I was introduced to the internet via WebTV in 1998. So, I'd like to give a big thank you to all the people who shared their cocktail-related tricks, trivia, and history with me.

Cheers! To Brenda Knight, Yaddyra Peralta, Natasha Vera, and Morgane Leoni at Mango Publishing. A well-deserved toast to my agent, June Clark at FinePrint Literary Management and a Champagne tower of thanks to my gracious cocktail friends who emailed me images for this book. Thank you, John, "JB" Bandy, Paul Harrington, Darcy O'Neil, Jamie Boudreau, Jared Brown, Anistatia Miller, Ocean Organic Vodka, Sean Kenyon, Ted A. Breaux, Brian Huff, Adam Elmegirab, Sobelman's Pub & Grill, Eau de Vie Bar, Joseph Ambrose, Gläce Luxury Ice, Jeff "Beachbum" Berry, Bobby "Robert" Lozoff, Diana Lehman, Neal Murray, Patrick "Paddy" Mitten, Cheryl Cook, Gosling's Black Seal rum, Dennis Oda, Lisa Laird, Camper English, Dale and Jill DeGroff, Natalie Bovis, Anthony Joseph Filippone, Tony Abou-Ganim, Christian Delpech, David Wondrich, Employees Only, Christy Pope, Chad Solomon, Tobin Ellis, H. Joseph Ehrmann, and Doc Eason.

Index

A

absinthe: 17, 22, 31, 84, 86-90, 127, 138, 141-142, 168

Absolut: 31, 54-55, 124-126

Akvavit: 75

Alabama Slammer: 142

Amaretto Sour: 73, 146

Amarula: 75

Americano: 80, 83, 85, 115, 139, 145

Ancho Reyes: 31, 74

Angostura bitters: 72, 91, 121, 134, 139-140, 144, 146-147

aperitifs: 83-84

Appletini: 73

Apricot Sour: 146

aqua vitae: 11, 68

armagnac: 11, 84

arrack: 11

Aviation: 59, 73, 110, 112, 116

Eric Alperin: 165

Joseph Ambrose: 169

B

Bacardi: 61-64, 78, 116, 156

Bahama Mama: 140

Baileys Irish Cream: 31, 73-74

Banshee: 120

bar tools: 22, 153, 156

Bay Breeze: 122

Beaujolais: 80, 82

Bellini: 116-117

Bénédictine: 74, 81, 144, 146

Between the Sheets: 117, 156

bitters: 16, 72, 91-96, 102, 121, 123, 134, 139-141, 144, 146-147, 157

black ants: 10, 110

Black Russian: 73, 117, 149

blanco tequila: 66, 132

Bloody Mary: 88, 98, 102, 108-109, 118

blue agave tequila: 66

Blue Hawaii: 119

Blue Hawaiian: 119

Blue Margarita: 133

Boilermaker: 76-77

Boker's bitters: 92

Bols: 57, 74, 119

Boston shaker: 114, 152-153

bottle opener: 153-154

Bourbon O Bar: 10, 90

Bramble: 113, 120

Brandy Alexander: 84, 120, 155

Brandy Crusta: 26, 121

Bubble Bath Martini: 111

Buck's Fizz: 135

Bushmills Irish whiskey: 15

Bushwhacker: 140

Jamie Boudreau: 47, 169

Jared Brown: 49, 169

John "JB" Bandy: 38, 164

Julio Bermejo: 145

Natalie Bovis: 169

Walter Bergeron: 146

C

Cable Car: 121

Caipirinha: 122

Campari: 83-84, 93, 115, 131, 139

CHERYL CHARMING

Cheryl Charming—a.k.a. Miss Charming™—began working in the food & beverage industry in 1976. At age sixteen, she took a job as a pizza waitress then quickly progressed to a cocktail waitress, barback, bartender, and head bartender. With a penchant for travel, Cheryl tended bar in nine American states, a cruise ship in the Caribbean, Walt Disney World, and Bourbon Street in New Orleans. While working at Walt Disney World, she became the bar trick and magic instructor for Disney's F&B training program, Quest for the Best.

Cheryl has hosted events for Tales of the Cocktail, studied graphic design at Ringling College of Art & Design, teaches cocktail classes, and for ten years designed cocktail menus for Brown-Forman. She is also the author of several books. *The Bartender's Ultimate Guide to Cocktails* is her seventeenth.

Currently, Miss Charming lives in the French Quarter and is the bar director at the Bourbon "O" Bar on Bourbon Street. In 2015, she held the *New Orleans Magazine* title of "Mixologist of the Year." She lives in a balcony apartment on Bourbon Street.

Mango Publishing, established in 2014, publishes an eclectic list of books by diverse authors—both new and established voices—on topics ranging from business, personal growth, women's empowerment, LGBTQ studies, health, and spirituality to history, popular culture, time management, decluttering, lifestyle, mental wellness, aging, and sustainable living. We were recently named 2019 *and* 2020's #1 fastest growing independent publisher by *Publishers Weekly.* Our success is driven by our main goal, which is to publish high quality books that will entertain readers as well as make a positive difference in their lives.

Our readers are our most important resource; we value your input, suggestions, and ideas. We'd love to hear from you—after all, we are publishing books for you!

Please stay in touch with us and follow us at:

Facebook: Mango Publishing
Twitter: @MangoPublishing
Instagram: @MangoPublishing
LinkedIn: Mango Publishing
Pinterest: Mango Publishing
Newsletter: mangopublishinggroup.com/newsletter

Join us on Mango's journey to reinvent publishing, one book at a time.